EFFECTIVE COUNSELLING WITH YOUNG PEOPLE

HAZEL REID AND JANE WESTERGAARD

Series editor: Norman Claringbull

LearningMatters

First published in 2011 by Learning Matters Ltd

British Library Cataloguing in Publication Data
A CIP record for this book is available from the British Library.

ISBN: 978 0 85725 295 1

This book is also available in the following ebook formats:

Adobe ebook   ISBN: 978 0 85725 297 5
ePUB ebook   ISBN: 978 0 85725 296 8
Kindle   ISBN: 978 0 85725 298 2

Cover design by Code 5 Design Associates
Project management by Diana Chambers
Typeset by Kelly Winter
Printed and bound in Great Britain by Short Run Press Ltd, Exeter, Devon

Learning Matters Ltd
20 Cathedral Yard
Exeter EX1 1HB
Tel: 01392 215560
info@learningmatters.co.uk
www.learningmatters.co.uk

FSC
www.fsc.org
MIX
Paper from
responsible sources
FSC® C014540

Contents

Foreword

Hazel Reid and Jane Westergaard are experienced teachers, knowledgeable trainers and, above all, skilled practitioners in the field of counselling young people. These are the very qualities that give them their academic and practice-based authority to 'tell it like it is' and to pass on their experience to the next generation of counsellors and psychotherapists who will be working with young people. This book is essential reading for anyone who is likely to engage in any form of therapeutic relationship with a young person.

A core principle set out in this book is that youth counselling is not just general counselling applied to young people, but a therapeutic discourse in its own right. The authors make the point that young people are still developing physically, emotionally and cognitively and so, psychologically, they are not merely 'mini-adults'. Young people have their own unique demands of the counselling and psychotherapy profession and, put simply, if they want to talk, then their therapists have to know how to listen.

It is a sad fact that the particular needs of the younger population are all too often ignored in most general counselling and psychotherapy textbooks. Moreover, many of the training programmes that are offered to therapists do not seem to adequately address the needs of young people. This lack has contributed to an erroneous default position, unwittingly held by all too many therapeutic practitioners, that 'one size fits all'. However, the authors of this book tackle this by constructively showing us some of the ways in which we might reconsider our therapeutic attitudes towards young people: they do not just ask us to think about what might be wrong; they encourage us to think hard about how to put it right.

From the outset, Hazel and Jane approach theoretical and practical counselling and psychotherapy, and its integration, from the perspective of the needs of our younger clients. That is what is so original about their writing. They guide us towards a new understanding of counselling and its applications for a new genre of potentially specialist counsellors and psychotherapists; those who will be working with the emergent new generations in our society. That is what makes this book so special.

This book is not a 'bossy' book. No one tells you what to think. The authors give you the information and then encourage you to put it all together in the way that best suits you and your clients. After all, as Hazel and Jane tell us so clearly, the needs of young people are infinitely varied and, therefore, so too must be the responses of their therapists. This book also highlights the fact that working with young people makes particular demands on counsellors and psychotherapists. Productive counselling with young people needs therapists who are sensitive to such clients' needs and who have a properly prepared theoretical and practical approach to their work.

So, if you want to know how to be an effective counsellor with young people and if you want to be able to usefully respond to their psychotherapeutic needs, then this is the perfect book for you.

Dr Norman Claringbull – Series editor
www.normanclaringbull.co.uk

About the authors

Hazel Reid is Reader in Career Guidance and Counselling and Director of the Centre for Career and Personal Development at Canterbury Christ Church University, UK. She teaches career counselling theory and research methods, and supervises a number of students undertaking Doctoral research. She has a particular interest in reflexive, narrative and biographic approaches in research that is related to education and the 'helping' services. Hazel is a Fellow of the Institute of Career Guidance and a Fellow of the National Institute of Careers Education and Counselling. She has published widely and presents her work at national and international conferences. She is involved in European projects connected to the work of career and school counsellors. Her previous research was concerned with the meanings given to the function of supervision within career counselling and youth support work. Currently she is exploring the development of constructivist approaches for integrative career counselling.

Jane Westergaard is a senior lecturer at Canterbury Christ Church University, UK. She teaches on a range of programmes specifically designed for students who plan to work with young people in a range of settings, but not in teaching roles. These youth support professionals include school counsellors, classroom assistants, learning mentors, careers advisers and personal advisers. Jane has a particular interest in counselling young people, working with young people in the group context and supervision. She has recently published a book on Effective Group Work with Young People. Jane has spoken on the subjects of counselling, supervision and group work at a number of national and international conferences. She is a qualified and practising UKRC (United Kingdom Register of Counsellors) registered counsellor, working with young people and adult clients.

Introduction

Why did we think writing this book was a good idea? More importantly, why did we think other people will think that writing this book was a good idea? We work, teach and research in sectors where the 'inclusion' of young people has resulted in a raft of policy interventions and changes in the way public services are organised. That's one reason. As importantly, we like working with young people and find the work stimulating, often challenging and deeply satisfying. In addition, an investment in young people and their 'health' – in the broadest terms – has led to the development of many para-professional roles to support young people, alongside colleagues who counsel young people or use counselling skills and approaches in their work.

So, before embarking on the writing we had a conversation where we questioned the need for a text that introduces readers to a range of approaches for counselling young people specifically. We felt we could justify why such a book was needed now and we were confident about our view that there is no one right way of 'doing' counselling. We believe that young people are diverse and need different approaches according to what they bring to counselling at different times. And we think that counsellors need to be flexible – what Cooper and McLeod (2010) term 'pluralistic' in their use of counselling methods. But we also raised questions about integrating aspects from different theoretical and practical orientations and about the dangers of a superficial understanding of a range of approaches. The conversation was helpful for us, so we rehearsed the issues again in preparation for writing this introductory chapter and this time recorded it. The transcript is included below as the response to the questions raised (for ease of reading we have removed all the ers and ums and other stumbles!).

WHY ARE WE WRITING THIS BOOK AND WHO IS IT FOR?

Hazel: 'So Jane, when we first talked about doing this book, remind me why we decided to write a book that has lots of chapters which are introducing people to these various theoretical approaches? Why are we doing that, rather than assuming people will go and read a book on, say, solution-focused counselling or cognitive behavioural therapy?'

Jane: 'I think we've written a book which really focuses on an integrative approach to working with young people. And, in order to engage with an integrative approach, we need to have an understanding of a range of theoretical perspectives, and of course, people could read books about solution-focused or multicultural counselling for instance; but what we've done in this book is to condense the key principles of those approaches . . .'

Hazel: 'Yes, quite.'

Jane: '. . . and we've also contextualised them specifically for those who are counselling or in helping relationships with young people. If the reader decides that they're particularly drawn to one approach, then of course they can and should read further. We provide them with lots of suggestions for further reading that they could do . . . but the idea was, I think, really to give them a starting point in terms of a) working with young people and b) understanding what an integrative approach is and how they might integrate from a range of approaches.'

Hazel: 'So, are we saying, then, that this is for people in training or beyond that?'

Jane: 'I think it is, clearly, for people in training because it does give them very much that starting point, but it's also for people who are beyond initial training, because what we do throughout the book is provide examples, activities, many of which ask the reader to reflect on their counselling practice. So I don't think at all that it's just limited to people who are training, although it would be very helpful for them. I think there's plenty in the book, plenty of meaty stuff for experienced counsellors to get their teeth into when practising.'

Hazel: 'And if they are in training, then they've got to be involved in practice in order to support the training.'

Jane: 'Absolutely.'

Hazel: 'OK, so how would we answer the criticism that what we're actually doing is . . . merely dipping our toe in, or to use the expression, that we're 'mining' from what are very deep and rich seams, but we're only surface-mining in those seams – we're not giving people a deep understanding?'

Jane: 'I think we answer that criticism by making it clear that that is what we are doing. In every chapter we have made the point that this is not a full and comprehensive text on a particular approach. But we are providing key principles, some ideas about how the techniques from the approaches covered can be used and integrated and, as I said before, we're providing ideas about additional reading . . . but I would still argue that a sound understanding – and I think that's what each of our chapters will provide – a sound understanding is better than no understanding at all . . . and therefore it is possible to use some solution-focused techniques, having read the chapter on solution-focused counselling, to use those in practice to good effect, because that chapter explains that there are also limitations to the approach, etc.'

Hazel: 'Yes, and I suppose the other thing that's in my mind is that . . . if you operate from a view point that you can only use one approach and you have to understand it in depth and fully, then you're setting up boundaries around what it's possible to do with people; and you're suggesting that this is the one way to do it. So what we're saying in terms of it being an integrative approach, is that what we're offering is an introduction to a number or a range of theories, methods, approaches, whatever word you want to use . . . in order to ensure that what you 'do' with your client is right for them . . . rather than only using the particular approach that you've been trained in (of course, there's always some element of personal appeal) . . . but we're saying that rather than put boundaries around different approaches, we'll let them, the approaches, 'talk' to each other a little bit and see what . . .'

Jane: 'Yes, quite, and I think it's particularly pertinent in work with young people because, for example, a pure person-centred approach may be very challenging for a young person and outside of their frame of reference and understanding. And it may be that the counselling is time-limited, so if you're counselling in a school, you may only have a number of sessions. Therefore we need to think more broadly than just one approach, I think, particularly with young people.'

Hazel: 'Hmm, the effect that this issue, this potential criticism, has had on me as I've written my chapters is that I feel as if I'm always apologising, almost. Yes, we say that we can't look at this in more depth because of the limitations of the chapter and so on, but I want to get beyond an apology for this, and I want the rationale for why we're doing this to be clear and quite robust.'

Jane: 'Yes, and my thinking about it is, for example – based on my experience as a counsellor of young people – is that they often bring or are referred with behavioural issues. Thus an understanding of things like CBT is really helpful to inform the work, and often they want to feel very actively involved – so solution-focused counselling is a good approach too. Again, the whole transactional analysis concept of ego states is really helpful for young people to understand how to communicate. So I think there is something about counselling with young people that makes it really important to be aware of different approaches and techniques. I know that you've said in a couple of chapters "if you're finding that something isn't working then it's helpful to try other things" but, of course, not in a kind of desperate "Help! Well what can I do now, I'll just try this", but in an informed way. So "now I have a relationship with this young person and I'm getting a greater understanding, maybe it would be helpful to try this approach".'

Hazel: 'Indeed. Sounds like theoretical integration . . . '

Jane: 'Exactly.'

Hazel: '. . . rather than using techniques without an understanding of what lies underneath them, the theory that underpins them, because that's where the danger lies.'

Jane: 'Yes.'

Hazel: 'OK, and just to finish this, who is this book for? We've said people who are counselling with young people, school counsellors and so on – who else?'

Jane: 'I think that it's much wider than that. Yes absolutely, first and foremost it's written for counsellors in training and counsellors working with young people, but I think there are a range of other professionals who could access this book and find it extremely helpful. I'm talking about those people involved in helping relationships with young people who are using counselling skills but who aren't trained to be counsellors. So, for example, personal advisers, learning mentors, those in educational welfare in its broadest sense, careers advisers and counsellors, of course: people who form those helping relationships with young people in a range of settings.'

Hazel: 'Yes, so then they could be in social justice, social work, some health care workers. OK, was there anything else that we would want to say in an introductory chapter? The introduction will go on to say what each of the chapters is about.'

Jane: 'And I'm sure you will say that each chapter could be 'standalone' – it could be that someone is particularly interested in just having an introduction to an approach and then they could read that particular chapter.'

Hazel: 'Yes, although the way we have structured the book is that we have placed some chapters at the start because we feel that they're important to read and to 'play' with a bit before you get into a range of approaches. But for somebody who's experienced it may be that they just wanted to look at motivational interviewing or narrative counselling, for example. Well, we've said that now so I'll not have to say it again in what follows!'

WHAT IS NOT INCLUDED IN THIS BOOK?

It may seem strange to write about what is not included, but we would want to clarify that a counsellor's education would require exploration of a range of introductory texts. For example, it is important to understand the historical development of counselling and what it aims to achieve (Claringbull, 2010; McLeod, 2009), the ethical, contractual and legal requirements of counselling (Bond, 2010; Daniels and Jenkins, 2010), the nature of the therapeutic relationship (Green, 2010), the need for reflective practice in counselling (Etherington, 2004) and the purpose and practices of supervision (Reid and Westergaard, 2006). When working in specific settings or with particular counselling needs, the work can be very complex and a developing expertise will be supported by reference to literature that offers insights into the area – for instance, when working with bereaved young people (Mallon, 2010). And, as Jane pointed out in the conversation above, new and experienced practitioners will want to access the latest research findings and developments in thinking. Continuous professional development will include reading professional journals and seeking out relevant articles in academic journals – the latter often have symposium issues around a theme relevant for particular work settings.

SO, WHAT IS INCLUDED IN THIS BOOK?

In addition to this introduction, there are nine other chapters. Chapters 1–4 deal with significant concepts that we feel underpin the later chapters. So, Chapter 1 outlines the key factors that impact on the physical, cognitive and psychological development of young people. Chapter 2 examines the development of an integrative approach to counselling young people, expanding the arguments begun in this introductory chapter. It identifies the principles underlying integration and introduces a model for structuring an integrative approach. Chapter 3 explores person-centred principles and counselling skills – these lie at the core of effective practice within an integrated approach. Chapter 4 looks at multicultural awareness and reflexive practice, in considering the range of social variables encountered in counselling.

In the remaining chapters specific approaches are introduced and explored. Transactional analysis (TA) is introduced in Chapter 5. TA can be used to offer an insight into the ways young people communicate and can encourage reflection on the consequences of a particular mode of communication. Chapter 6 considers how ideas from cognitive behavioural therapy can inform counselling practice with young people. It demonstrates how CBT has much to offer the youth counsellor when working alongside clients to effect change. Chapters 7, 8 and 9 introduce the reader to constructivist approaches within counselling. The concept is explained earlier in Chapter 4, but these chapters look at particular approaches, namely – motivational interviewing in Chapter 7, solution-focused approaches in Chapter 8 and a narrative approach in Chapter 9. There are similarities in these approaches, but also distinctions and (like all the chapters in this book) these are explored and 'unpacked' via case studies and other activities.

REFLECTION POINT

- What are your thoughts at this point about integration? Having considered this beforehand, take the opportunity to discuss with colleagues the potential advantages and disadvantages of integration.

FINAL INTRODUCTORY WORDS

This is not the only book dedicated to counselling young people and other texts are drawn on within the chapters mentioned above. Like other books in this Learning Matters series, the chapters examine the relevant theory but are practical in focus in order to clarify the links between theoretical concepts and everyday practice. Jane and I work well together and have been each other's 'critical friend'. When commenting on drafts we have been able to indicate when our understanding of each other's writing would benefit from a bit of re-wording or a practical activity to aid learning. For example, Jane would write, 'I'm glad there was a case study here as I was beginning to struggle a bit with this concept – perhaps an activity or a little more explanation earlier on would be good?' or I would suggest, 'I'm wondering if it would be useful to ask the reader to write something here as, if they are like me, they'll skip a reflection point unless asked to think a bit deeper and do something with those thoughts?' So, we have learnt from each other and enjoyed the collaboration involved in writing the text. We hope enjoyment accompanies your learning in the use of this book.

SUGGESTED FURTHER READING

Claringbull, N (2010) *What is Counselling and Psychotherapy?* Exeter: Learning Matters.

As part of Learning Matters' Counselling and Psychotherapy Practice series, the book is written specifically to support students at the beginning stage of their counselling. It covers the development of counselling and psychotherapy and the multiplicity of theoretical approaches, and the move to integrative models. The work is accessible and digestible – engaging the reader through the use of activities, practical examples and case studies.

McLeod, J (2009) *An Introduction to Counselling*, 4th edition. Berks, UK: McGraw Hill/Open University Press.

Previous editions have been influential in the development of our understanding and practice and are used in our writing for this book. As a recommendation, it is sensible to point readers to this, the fourth edition – testament to its reputation as a key text. It is comprehensive, thorough and extensive with further updates. Despite being a 'weighty' book, it is enlivened throughout with short examples or case studies.

CHAPTER 1

Understanding adolescent development

by Jane Westergaard

CORE KNOWLEDGE

By the end of this chapter you will have the opportunity to:

- identify the key stages of physical development in adolescence;
- explain the significance of cognitive development in adolescence;
- consider the impact of a range of psychological and emotional factors during adolescence;
- reflect on the implications of adolescent development when counselling young people.

INTRODUCTION

The period known as 'adolescence' is perhaps one of the most turbulent, unsettling, yet exciting that we experience in our lives. The gradual move from a state of dependence on parental and authority figures and the relative 'safety' of childhood, to separation and the independence and autonomy of adulthood can be an uncertain journey. This journey can be fraught with hidden dangers, pitfalls and challenges. Significant changes are taking place, and the consequences of these physical, cognitive and emotional developments during adolescence are likely to have an impact on the decisions that young people make about the way in which they live their lives. It is, therefore, important that counsellors working with young people gain an understanding of the key factors that have an impact on the physical, cognitive and psychological development of the young people with whom they engage.

So, before this book moves on to examine specific approaches to counselling practice in detail, this chapter provides a brief introduction to those key elements of adolescent development identified above. As might be expected, there is a plethora of texts which investigate this fascinating and complex area in some depth (Piaget, 1954; Bowlby, 1969; Kohlberg, 1984; Steinberg, 1996; Coleman and Hendry, 1999; Kaplan, 2004; Christie and Viner, 2005;

Allen and Sheeber, 2008; Boyd and Bee, 2009). It is simply not possible to explore the subject in the same depth here. But what is provided, it is hoped, is a helpful 'overview' which could act as a starting point for more detailed investigation into the subject of adolescent growth and development. In addition, the chapter offers some insight into how these physical, cognitive and emotional developments through adolescence are a powerful and significant feature affecting the lives of all young people. The changes that happen at this time will often play a part in influencing and underpinning the issues that young people present in the counselling room.

This chapter starts by identifying the features of physical development which take place in adolescence. It goes on to detail key cognitive changes and finally the chapter examines aspects of adolescent emotional and psychological development. The chapter (like all those in this book) invites you to reflect on how your understanding of adolescent development illuminates and informs your counselling practice.

ACTIVITY 1.1

First, let us take a moment to try to recall what was happening to us in our own adolescence. Reflect on and note down your thoughts under the following headings.

- Between what ages would you say your 'adolescence' took place?
- How long did your adolescence last?
- What physical changes took place, and at what age?
- How did your thinking about things change?
- What were the most important events in your life at this time?
- Who were the most significant people in your life?
- Write down five key words to sum up your overriding feelings about yourself during this time.

Of course, for every individual who undertakes this activity, there will be a different response. For some, reflections on adolescence may be painful; for others, recalling that time may engender a warm, hazy glow. For most of us, this period of our lives is likely to produce ambivalent feelings – some positive, others less so. What will almost certainly be true for all is that our adolescence was a distinct and significant time in our lives.

PHYSICAL DEVELOPMENT

During adolescence, our bodies develop and change more visibly perhaps than at any other point in our lives. This can be a welcome and exciting change, but is nonetheless daunting at times. The changes we experience in body shape and a move towards sexual maturity suggest that 'I am now an adult' when, for many young people, their emotional and cognitive processes are yet to develop fully. Furthermore, for some young people, adolescence (in terms of physical development) can take place in as little as 18 months, while for others, the process can last up to five years. For numbers of young people this can be unsettling. They see their peers showing the distinctive signs of adulthood, while they still, to all intents and purposes, feel as though they inhabit the body of a child.

Christie and Viner (2005) suggest key biological 'tasks of adolescence' through which all young people should develop. The tasks are summarised in Table 1.1.

As this table shows, the pituitary gland is responsible for 'kick-starting' these physical changes and its significance should not be underestimated. Indeed, McMaster and Kusumakar (2004) suggest that there is a link between

Stage	Boys	Girls
Early adolescence (11–12)	Growth of genitals, triggered by the pituitary gland secreting the testosterone hormone.	Development of breast buds and growth of pubic hair, onset of growth spurt, triggered by the pituitary gland secreting the hormone estradiol (a form of oestrogen).
Mid-adolescence (13–14)	Onset of growth spurt, first experiences of ejaculation (spermarche), voice breaks, growth of pubic and facial hair.	End of growth spurt, onset of periods (menarche), more rounded body shape as fat is deposited.
Late adolescence (15+)	End of body spurt, changes in body shape, increased muscle, body and facial hair continuing to grow.	Puberty normally at an end.

Table 1.1 Physical development in adolescence

depression in adolescence and dysfunction in the pituitary gland. This is not the sole reason that 18–30 per cent of adolescents experience depression (Saluja et al., 2004); a range of complex issues play a part, but it *is* a contributing *physical* factor. As can also be seen from the table above, although both boys and girls experience a growth spurt in adolescence, there is a difference between the sexes in terms of when this growth takes place. In most cases, girls experience their growth spurt earlier (on average by two years) than their male peers. Tanner (1970) suggests that girls in early adolescence are likely to be both taller and heavier than boys of the same age. However, usually by the age of 13 or 14, boys will be 'catching up' with their female peers while 'adult height' is normally reached between the ages of 15 and 16 for girls, and 16 and 18 for boys (Brooks-Gunn and Petersen, 1984).

What is clear is that significant physical change takes place over a relatively short time for both boys and girls. This, of course, is likely to have an emotional and psychological impact on young people and this will be examined later in the chapter. It is important to recognise that these changes will also have practical consequences. For example, the period of the growth spurt uses up significant amounts of energy. Ideally, at this time, young people should be sleeping for at least nine hours a night. However, many young people do not sleep for as long as they need. This is an increasing worry, particularly with the advent of computer games, social networking sites and so on, which are often nocturnal activities. In addition, girls starting their periods will need to prepare for and 'manage' their monthly bleeding. This can be a difficult and sometimes embarrassing experience as the menstrual cycle can take time to establish, and the regularity and severity of bleeding may change from month to month. Boys will also have to deal with the practical consequences of nocturnal emissions (more commonly known as wet dreams). Kaplan makes an interesting point concerning this particular physical development:

> *Psychologists know little about the meaning of puberty to boys. Is the occurrence of ejaculation, the expulsion of semen from the penis, as significant for boys as menarche is for girls? Boys receive little information about ejaculation from any source. In fact, boys may actually know more about menarche than about ejaculation.*
>
> (2004, p65)

Kaplan goes on to suggest that:

> *Boys are very reluctant to discuss the experience with parents or even friends, and when they do, it is in the form of humour.*
>
> (2004, p65)

REFLECTION POINT

- Think about the young people you have been working with recently. What kind of issues have they brought to counselling, which, on reflection, are underpinned or influenced by the physical changes that are taking place?

It is likely that, even if at first glance, presenting problems do not appear to be directly connected to the physical changes that take place in adolescence, on closer examination a link can often be found. Geldard and Geldard summarise this point neatly:

These physiological changes occur over a period of time. They happen at different ages and different rates for different young people. Consequently there may be issues for the adolescent who may feel embarrassed, self-conscious, awkward and out of step with their peers who are developing at a different rate. It is therefore not surprising that many adolescents become very anxious about their appearance.

(2004, p5)

They go on to explain further:

Biological changes clearly present the adolescent with major challenges. The adolescent has to cope with body changes, which may be disturbing and worrying, and with the emergence of sexual urges that drive the young person into the exploration of new relationships which themselves produce new sexual challenges.

(2004, p6)

Clearly, there is a link to be made between the physical changes that are taking place in adolescence and possible issues brought to counselling. The case study outlined below, concerning **Carla**, demonstrates this.

Case study 1.1   Carla

Carla is 14 years old. She is one of the eldest in her year group at school – most of her friends are still 13. She has been referred to her school counsellor because teachers have expressed concerns about her behaviour, which has changed dramatically in the last few months. Where Carla has always been an attentive, hardworking, positive, outgoing and popular student, she has now become unfocused, disruptive in class and aggressive towards other classmates and some teachers.

Carla is very small for her age and has not yet developed physically into adolescence. Recently, most of Carla's friends have had their growth spurt and have changed physically from girls into young women. Much of the talk in Carla's friendship group is about boyfriends, going out, clothes and make-up. Carla does not feel part of this. Her mum still buys her clothes in children's clothes shops. Where once Carla was a natural dominant member of her friendship group, her status with her friends appears to have changed. She seems to be on the periphery of the group, slightly detached and out of place.

At her first counselling session, Carla presents initially as defiant and angry. She can't understand why she has been referred to see a counsellor. However, it is not long in the first session before Carla's defences collapse and she becomes visibly upset, describing herself as 'abnormal'. She expresses deep-seated anxiety about her size, worried that she will never 'grow up' like her friends. She feels excluded from their conversations and wants to regain her status within the group.

COMMENT

Clearly, Carla's lack of physical development is of real concern to her. Although every young person develops in their own time at their own pace, being a few months 'behind' your peer group can feel like an eternity during adolescence. In Carla's case, this early lack of development appears to be having an impact on her behaviour as she finds alternative ways to attract the attention of her friends and regain the status she previously enjoyed in her group.

As already suggested, it is not only the body that develops in adolescence. The development of the brain and the way that young people think also changes, making space for thoughts about previously unfamiliar abstract concepts like morality, sexual identity and, perhaps, religious and political ideology. Like physical development, the emergence of new ways of thinking can be an empowering, but also a challenging and sometimes frightening experience for young people.

COGNITIVE DEVELOPMENT

The ideas of Piaget (1954) provide a useful starting point for understanding how cognition develops in adolescence. Although Piaget's work has been developed further and contested at times, (Elkind, 1967; Shayer and Wylam, 1978; Turiel, 1978; Selman, 1980; Barenboim, 1981) it is nevertheless widely referred to in the literature and is worthy of mention here.

Piaget focused his studies on changes in the ways in which children and young people think about and respond to problems. He used a clinical approach to investigate these developments, setting up experiments aimed at testing changes in cognition. As a result he identified a number of different stages of cognitive development:

- sensorimotor stage (birth to 24 months);
- preoperational stage (2 to 7 years);
- concrete operations (7 to 11 years);
- formal operations (11 years onwards).

It is not necessary to explore *each* stage in detail here, as it is the 'formal operations' stage that is of particular interest to those who work with young people. Piaget proposed that a number of key changes in the ways in which we think and process information take place at this stage. He identified five cognitive abilities which he suggested become evident in adolescents and adults, but are not present in younger children. Kaplan (2004) describes these in detail. In brief, these five abilities are as follows.

1 Separating the real from the possible – developing the ability to think about alternatives and possibilities. *This can lead to questioning and dissatisfaction on the part of some young people who can begin to picture an alternative reality to the one that they inhabit.*
2 Hypothetical-deductive logic – the ability to construct a hypothesis about a situation, event or circumstances. *This can help young people to think more rationally, question and make sense of concepts that they have previously accepted as 'given'.*
3 Combinational logic – the ability to acknowledge a number of possible solutions to a problem. A realisation that there is more than 'one way' of doing things. *This is significant as during adolescence, young people are presented with key decisions regarding their present and future lives. An awareness that there is more than one option available is helpful.*
4 Abstract, symbolic thought – occurring between 13 and 15 years of age, young people develop an understanding of abstract concepts such as religious or political thought. *It is important that young people access this ability and begin to develop their own moral principles, beliefs and values.*
5 Thinking about thinking – the ability to develop reflection and analysis of their own thoughts and actions. *This is particularly significant in counselling, as counsellors will be inviting young people to reflect on and understand their thoughts, feelings and behaviour at a deeper level.*

> ### ACTIVITY 1.2
>
> - Think about one or two of the young people with whom you are working. Note down examples of evidence of the five stages detailed above (for example, what is it specifically that the young person has said or done that suggests they are developing these cognitive abilities)?

Sometimes, this new way of *relativist* thinking can be challenging for young people. They begin to realise that the knowledge they have developed is based on their own experiences of life thus far, and is not necessarily a universally held truth. Counsellors will often be faced with 'I don't know' or 'it depends' reactions from their clients, when responding to the invitation to reflect on and think critically about an issue. Perhaps, as Keating (1991) and Leadbetter (1991) suggest, at this time young people begin to question whether there is such a thing as an 'answer' to anything. If this is true, it is likely to add to the young person's anxiety about the new and uncertain world in which they live.

Geldard and Geldard (2004) also propose five key changes in cognition in adolescence. Like Piaget (1977) and Kaplan (2004), they suggest that young people develop the ability to think in a more abstract, less concrete way. The five 'categories' of change they propose are likely to resonate with counsellors (and others) who come into close contact with young people.

- **Thinking egocentrically** – young people often have a sense that everything revolves around them. Feelings of being watched, a sense of being misunderstood, uniqueness, and, at times, omnipotence, all create the impression for young people that no one else will be able to understand how they really feel.
- **Thinking about others** – in spite of the predisposition towards egocentric thinking described above, young people also begin to develop an awareness and understanding of how to think about and 'make sense of' others. This helps them in the development of relationships.
- **Thinking using information** – young people begin to develop strategies to use and remember information that they consider to be of use to them. This can help them to make decisions in an informed, rational way.
- **Thinking critically** – this capacity links to the ability outlined above. Not only do young people develop the capacity to use and remember information they receive, but they also begin to be able to think critically and *process* information, thoughts and feelings. This helps to

inform judgements, conclusions and decisions on which young people act.

- **Thinking creatively** – young people begin to develop the ability to think in divergent ways, to consider a range of possibilities and to accept that there is often more than one answer to a problem or a number of options available to consider in any given situation.

The overwhelming conclusion drawn from Piaget's, Kaplan's and Geldard and Geldard's analysis of changes in cognition is that adolescents begin to develop key life-changing thinking abilities. They are able to understand that their lives are not straightforward but are complex. They develop the ability to realise that there is often no single solution to a problem. They know that how they think and what they do is likely to have an impact on others. Most importantly of all, they develop the realisation that they are becoming increasingly responsible for the decisions they make about their lives. This is all highly significant for the work of the counsellor, whose role is to use this knowledge in order to challenge young people and encourage all their clients to reflect on and think creatively about their lives.

The example of counselling practice below shows **Paul**, a mental health counsellor, working with **Leo**, a sixteen-year-old young man who has been experiencing panic attacks. The example demonstrates how the counsellor's awareness of Leo's cognitive development provides an opportunity to invite Leo to think critically and creatively about his situation.

Case study 1.2 Paul and Leo

Paul: 'So you seem to be making a link between the panic attacks you've been experiencing recently and a particular situation that you often find yourself in?'

Leo: 'Yes, definitely. I've realised, since I've been coming here to talk to you, that these feelings of panic often happen when I'm due to meet up with my mates. You know, going out, a party or something like that. It's ridiculous. You'd think if I'm going to get anxious it would be because of stress at school, course work, or my parents stressing me out. Not something good like meeting my mates.'

Paul: 'Yes, it's interesting isn't it? And I wonder why it seems there's a connection between your feelings of panic and going out with your mates? What do you think that's all about?'

Leo (hesitantly): 'Erm . . . I don't know really. I've got no idea.'

Paul (leaving a silence): 'What do you think it *might* be? Why might going out with friends raise your levels of anxiety?'

Leo: 'I'm not sure really. I can't think of a reason. I'm not aware of anything . . . '

Paul: 'OK. Well, let's have a think about some of the reasons why other people might feel anxious about going out with their friends. What might they be?'

Leo: 'I dunno. I guess if something bad has happened before, when you've been out with them. Like if your mates have got into trouble, into a fight or something like that?'

Paul: 'Yes, exactly, good. Anything else? Any other reasons?'

Leo: 'Well, maybe if you don't want to do the things that your friends want, but you are just going along for the ride. You know, you might feel pressured.'

Paul: 'OK, good,' (pause) 'and have you ever found yourself in those situations?'

Leo: 'Well, no,' (silence) 'well not recently. I mean, it only happened once and that was a while ago now.'

Paul: 'How would it feel to talk about it now? Maybe it would help. It might even go some way to explaining what's happening to you now. What do you think?'

Leo: 'Alright, then. Well, what happened was this . . .'

ACTIVITY 1.3

• In case study 1.2, how is Paul using his knowledge of adolescent cognitive development to encourage Leo to reflect on possible triggers for his panic attacks? For example, which of Geldard and Geldard's five cognitive abilities is he inviting Leo to use?

Note how Paul takes the focus away from Leo by exploring 'why *other people* might feel anxious'.

COMMENT

Counsellors working with young people should be cognisant of the ways in which thinking develops in adolescence. Having access to this knowledge will enable counsellors to encourage critical and creative reasoning in their clients, just as Paul has done in the example above. Furthermore, this knowledge will provide an additional perspective which young people can reflect on, process and use to make sense of their world and the ways in which others respond to them.

In addition to physical developments and changes in cognition in adolescence, young people are also burdened with new and hitherto unfamiliar feelings. As with physical and cognitive changes, this psychological development can be exciting, strange or even frightening at times. So, what are these new emotions and how might they have an impact on young people's lives?

EMOTIONAL DEVELOPMENT

At the beginning of this chapter you were asked to undertake a reflective activity, focusing on your own development through adolescence. You were invited to select five words to sum up your feelings about yourself at that time. My guess is that the words you chose were powerful, possibly ambivalent, and, when you undertook the activity, those feelings were likely to have come flooding back. For some, the feelings would have been positive, for others they would have been negative. For most of us, the emotions associated with adolescence would be both – positive and negative. For all of us, the feelings are likely to have been *influential* in our lives at the time. Rosenblum and Lewis explain that:

> *Adolescent emotional experience is in part a function of the incorporation of new cognitive and physiological events and the influence on the adolescents' perceptions of their development.*
>
> (2003, p269)

Boyd and Bee (2009) describe the importance of young people developing self-understanding or a *self-concept* in adolescence. They explain that it is during adolescence when we begin to recognise that we fulfil a number of roles in our lives. For example, in the life of a young woman – daughter, friend, pupil, sister and other roles – and it is partly by developing our understanding of these roles that we can begin to shape our *identity*.

For many young people the establishment of identity is likely to be an emotional task, often involving turmoil or upheaval (Arnett, 1999). Erikson (1968) stresses the importance of working towards achieving this identity in adolescence. Marcia (1966, 1980) develops this thinking about identity further and suggests four *identity statuses*. Boyd and Bee describe these as follows.

- *Identity achievement*: *The person has been through a crisis and has reached a commitment to ideological, occupational or other goals.*
- *Moratorium*: *a crisis in progress, but no commitment has yet been made.*
- *Foreclosure*: *The person has made a commitment without having gone through a crisis. No reassessment of old positions has been made. Instead, the young person has simply accepted a parentally or culturally defined commitment.*
- *Identity diffusion*: *The young person is not in the midst of a crisis (although there may have been one in the past) and has not made a commitment. Diffusion may thus represent an early stage in the process (before a crisis) or a failure to reach a commitment after a crisis.*

(2009, p342)

Clearly, the statuses above are linked, to some extent, to the development of cognition, but they are also, in large part, informed by the emotional development of the young person. Rosenblum and Lewis (1999) make this link between cognitive and emotional development clear. The 'crisis' referred to in each status detailed above is likely to involve 'feelings' as well as cognitions about certain situations and aspects of a young person's life. Christie and Viner (2005) set out to explain these key crises or 'challenges' of adolescence. They suggest a number of challenges faced by young people which are likely to engender a range of emotional responses. These are:

- challenging authority;
- taking risks;
- experimentation (for example, drugs, alcohol, clothes, identity, sex);
- challenging society;
- demanding their rights;
- taking responsibility (for self and others);
- looking for spiritual options;
- transitions in education;
- moving into employment;
- new relationships with peers;
- developing a sexual identity;
- renegotiating relationships and authority at home.

Any counsellor who has worked with young people will not be surprised by the tasks or challenges listed here. The struggle to overcome these challenges and develop an identity is often at the heart of the complex and emotionally charged issues brought by young people to counselling. Familiar as the challenges listed above are to those who work closely with young people, some are nevertheless worthy of deeper reflection. In particular, the ways in which young people respond to the challenges of risk-taking and experimentation are a central aspect of emotional development into adulthood. But the extent to which risks are taken and the level of experimentation in relation to potentially harmful activities, can often raise the anxiety levels of those who work with, or care for young people. Boyd and Bee explain further:

> *Teenagers appear to have what many developmentalists describe as a heightened level of sensation-seeking, or a desire to experience increased levels of arousal such as those that accompany fast driving or the 'highs' associated with drugs. Sensation-seeking leads to recklessness, which, in turn, leads to markedly increased rates of accidents and injuries in this age range.*
>
> (2009, p318)

Counsellors working with young people often find themselves faced with descriptions of behaviours, influenced by emotional imperatives, which are negative or even harmful. It is important that they use supervision in order to reflect on the tensions that may exist between establishing a relationship of trust, where the young person feels safe enough to share difficult or even dangerous material with their counsellor, and the consequences of such behaviour.

Another challenge from the list above which is worthy of note is that of developing a sexual identity. This is another task of adolescence that is likely to be underpinned by a range of emotional responses in young people; fear, excitement, shame, embarrassment and confusion, to name a few. When faced with young people who are experiencing these powerful emotional responses concerning their sexual development, it is important to remind ourselves that sexuality does not develop in a vacuum. Therefore, the feelings that young people are experiencing are likely to have been influenced in a number of ways by a range of factors, including books and magazines, film, TV and other web-based media, peers, social and religious groups and, perhaps most importantly, the family. On the subject of an emerging gay, lesbian or bi-sexual identity, for example, Coleman and Hendry explain that:

> *The role of parents is critical in allowing an individual to come to terms with their sexual identity. Here, again, there is a great need to tackle the ignorance which surrounds this subject, in order that young people may be able to disclose their sexuality to their parents without encountering the stereotypes and prejudices still pervasive in our society.*
>
> (1999, p111)

These challenges of adolescence are neither simple, straightforward nor easily negotiated for many young people. Add to the mix the increased *levels* of emotion experienced by adolescents and there is likely to be significant amounts of rich material to work with, in the counselling room. Larson et al. (1980) undertook research that supports the view that adolescence is characterised by greater extremes of emotion than adulthood. Geldard and Geldard summarise:

> *Stimuli of relatively minor significance for most adults may result in significant mood swings for the adolescent who may respond with unexpectedly high levels of emotion including excitement, anger, sadness, depression and embarrassment. Adolescents clearly have a difficult time dealing with the heightened intensity of their emotions and reactions.*
>
> (2004, p10)

REFLECTION POINT

- Make a list of as many emotions as you can that have been expressed by young people in the counselling room. When you think about the young people you have worked with recently, can you identify any negative emotions that are 'common' or explored more frequently in your work?

Two common negative emotions that are prevalent in adolescence, both of which, I suspect, appeared on your list, are those of shame and anger. These two powerful emotions are often related. Many young people experience feelings of shame in relation to different areas of their lives; how they look, how they feel, what they say and how they behave. Often these feelings of shame are heavily disguised as anger, in order to defend or detract from the real and painful emotional response of shame, humiliation or embarrassment that they are experiencing. The case study below, focusing on 14-year-old **Natalie** and her counsellor **Kate**, illustrates this.

Case study 1.3 Kate and Natalie

Kate: 'You seem quite angry today, Natalie, and a bit fed up. Have I got that right?'

Natalie: 'No!'

Kate: 'Oh. Well . . . I don't know . . . it's just that you are sitting slumped in your chair and you don't seem to want to look at me today. It feels like something isn't quite right.'

Natalie (defensively): 'Does it? I don't know why you think that.'

Kate: 'So . . . how *are* you feeling today?'

Natalie: 'I don't know. I'm OK. I suppose.'

Kate: 'You are OK, you suppose?'

Natalie (angrily): 'That's what I said, didn't I?'

Kate: 'Has something happened, Natalie?'

Natalie (silence): 'Maybe. But I don't want to talk to you about it, OK?'

Kate: 'That's fine, Natalie. But it feels like a pretty big thing that has happened. Maybe it would help to talk about it . . .?'

Natalie: 'Alright, if you insist. It's just that I've had a row with my mum. That's all.'

Kate: 'OK. And can you say what the row was about?'

Natalie: 'No!' (silence): 'Well alright, then. If you must know, my mum caught me nicking money out of her purse. OK? Satisfied?'

Natalie is presenting as a very angry young woman to her counsellor. But the anger is being used as a 'smoke screen' on this occasion, probably to disguise her shame at what she has done. The replacement of one emotion with another is not unusual. Sadness often takes the place of anger and vice versa, excitement often camouflages fear, insecurity can be portrayed as bravado, aggression can mask self-loathing and fear is sometimes expressed as jealousy. This is not a conscious attempt at 'game playing' on the part of young people, but rather a subconscious strategy to deal with difficult and painful emotions.

ACTIVITY 1.4

Try to identify one or two clients with whom you have worked, who have presented with a powerful emotion, which, when examined more closely, is disguising another equally or even more powerful feeling. Consider the questions below and write down your responses.

- What was the presenting emotion?
- What was the underlying feeling?
- How did you work with this in counselling?
- What would you have done differently (if anything) having read this chapter?

This emotional aspect of adolescent development is both complex and critical to successful progression towards adulthood. The role of the counsellor here is to help young people to identify, own and explore their emotions; to consider the impact their feelings have on their thoughts and their behaviour and, most importantly, to reassure young people that the intensity of their emotional responses is a normal part of adolescence.

CHAPTER SUMMARY

This chapter set out to examine some of the key features of adolescent development of which those who work with young people should be aware. What has become clear is that adolescence is a complex, often confusing, sometimes frightening, and frequently exciting time. This is a relatively short period in our lives which has a significant and often unforgettable impact. We are not only changing physically, but also our thinking and emotions are undergoing development. How effectively the journey is managed from childhood to adulthood through the transition phase of adolescence will shape the rest of our lives. With a 'good enough' level of support and understanding from parents, carers, friends and others, a smooth transition can be achieved. However, support may be lacking or events may occur which provide a barrier to an effective transition to adulthood. At times such as these, the services of a counsellor may be sought. The remainder of this book will focus on ways in which counsellors can support this period of potential turmoil and enable young people to mature into the adult person they would like to be.

SUGGESTED FURTHER READING

Adams, GR and Berzonsky, MD (eds) (2003) *Blackwell Handbook of Adolescence.* Malden, MA: Blackwell.

A selection of useful and enlightening chapters written by specialists in the field, dealing with a broad range of issues relating to adolescence.

Boyd, D and Bee, H (2009) *Lifespan Development,* 5th edition. Boston: Pearson.

Part V of this book focuses specifically on adolescent development. It draws on a wealth of research in the field and presents this in a coherent and easily digested form.

Kaplan, PS (2004) *Adolescence.* Boston: Houghton Mifflin.

An interactive text which explains ideas simply and engages the reader in activities to develop understanding further.

Sudbery, J (2010) *Human Growth and Development.* London: Routledge.

Chapters 1–4 focus specifically on the development of children and adolescents.

Viner, R (ed.) (2005) *ABC of Adolescence.* Massachusetts: Blackwell Publishing.

This is a very easy to read, short, but informative book, neatly illustrated.

CHAPTER 2

Examining an integrative approach to counselling young people

by Jane Westergaard

CORE KNOWLEDGE

By the end of the chapter you will have the opportunity to:

- identify the key principles underpinning an integrative approach to counselling young people;
- consider the pros and cons of adopting an integrative approach with young people;
- establish a model for integrative counselling;
- examine how an integrative approach is applied in practice;
- reflect on the use of integration in your own practice.

INTRODUCTION

Most of us live our lives and make important decisions about them by adhering to a range of complex principles and concepts. We are influenced in our thinking, decision making and action by a number of factors including our own experiences, our values and beliefs, our feelings, our socio-cultural-economic background, our education, our gender, our sexuality, and so on.

At any one time, when it becomes clear that a decision about our lives is required, we assess the situation in which we find ourselves and consider the best way of approaching and dealing with the issues we face. Sometimes we may decide to take direct, concrete, practical action, based on an analysis of the pros and cons of particular options. On other occasions, perhaps where options are less clear cut, consequences are more complex and emotions are heightened; further introspection, reflection and exploration is required before any decisions can be made. Sometimes, particularly in adolescence where a world of opportunity and possibility is emerging, decision making may be less analytical and more impulsive, or even seemingly ill-informed and irrational. There may also be times in our lives when we find it impossible to take any action at all even though we are keen to make changes. Most people would argue that they do not live their lives by one set of rigid and inflexible rules, but rather respond pragmatically (or even irrationally at times), applying different knowledge, skills and expertise to inform decisions and make changes where necessary.

In other words, our decisions about our lives are formed by *integrating* a complex range of concepts, principles, experiences and reflections into our thinking, and then taking action as appropriate.

In many ways, an *integrative approach to counselling* mirrors what we already know and do in our lives. In brief, integrative counsellors draw from and integrate a range of theoretical perspectives in their counselling practice. Integrative counsellors are assisted in their practice by a range of integrative models, developed in recent years, which provide a sound theoretical under-pinning to the work. Clarkson's (2003) therapeutic relationship model, Culley and Bond's (2004) integrative skills approach, Geldard and Geldard's (2004) proactive approach, Evans and Gilbert's (2005) relational-develop-mental theory and Egan's (2007) skilled helper model, are each worthy of note (and additional reading relating to these is suggested at the end of this chapter). Opportunity to explore each of these approaches in detail is limited, but further examination of one of these – Egan's model – will take place later in the chapter.

As in a single theoretical approach (for example, person-centred, cognitive behavioural or solution-focused counselling and others), integrative coun-sellors working with young people place an emphasis on the quality of the counsellor–client relationship and begin their work by developing a relationship of trust whereby clients are enabled to identify and explore their issues and concerns in a safe environment. Once this assessment of individual needs takes place, the integrative counsellor's practice differs from those counsellors who adhere to a single approach. The integrative coun-sellor will consider possible ways of enabling their client to tackle issues by applying appropriate therapeutic perspectives to their counselling practice. These perspectives are drawn from the counsellor's knowledge of a range of counselling approaches. The integrative counsellor applies concepts and techniques that are most appropriate and 'fit' their assessment of the young person and their presenting problem and underlying issues. The purpose of integrative counselling is focused on working towards change; helping clients to reflect on the issues and problems they are facing in their lives so that they can examine and select appropriate courses of action.

Rather than using a single approach, integrative counsellors have a broad knowledge of key counselling concepts from which to select; they under-stand the principles of a range of theoretical orientations and value the differences in approach, while acknowledging the particular strengths and possible weaknesses of applying each theory to practice. Of course, this opens up the potential criticism 'jack of all trades, master of none', which will be addressed later. Geldard and Geldard explain that:

> *The advantage of such an integrative approach is that it increases the counsellor's repertoire in such a way that it is possible to address the needs and problems of particular clients more effectively by offering more options for intervention than a traditional single approach.*
>
> (2009, p22)

O'Brien and Houston agree that:

> *An integrative psychotherapy offers a student from the beginning a variety of approaches and encourages a critical and evaluative stance. In this way the therapist is able to develop her own favoured approach derived from a broad theoretical base and tested and modified through practice.*
>
> (2000, p19)

In terms of counselling approaches, the integrative counsellor's motto is, perhaps: rule nothing out!

REFLECTION POINT

In the Introductory chapter to this book you were asked to reflect on the concept of integration and to discuss it with colleagues.

- How much does this brief description resonate with your own practice and with any discussion that you were able to have?

If you have been trained in the integrative approach, what you have read so far will simply reinforce what you already know. If, however, you have been trained in a single counselling approach, you may find that you have questions and reservations about how integration might work in practice. Hopefully, some of those questions are addressed in what follows.

This chapter is the first in the book to introduce a particular approach to counselling. The remaining chapters follow a similar pattern, each examining a specific theoretical orientation and considering how and when the approach might be applied in practice. But it is by no means an accident that integration has been selected as a starting point. It is by offering an integrationist perspective to begin with, that the reader can consider the approaches that follow in a holistic way, analysing when and how each approach might be integrated into their counselling practice with young people.

The chapter now continues with an outline of the integrative approach and examines the pros and cons of adopting such an approach with young people. It goes on to introduce one of the integrative models referred to earlier in the chapter, which can be applied effectively in counselling practice (Egan, 2007). Furthermore, it explores how the approach can be applied to counselling practice with young people. Case studies are used throughout the chapter to bring the approach to life, and readers are encouraged to reflect on their own counselling orientation by considering the questions and activities that are posed at key points.

WHAT IS AN INTEGRATIVE APPROACH?

An integrative approach, as suggested above, is one whereby the counsellor understands, values and accesses a range of different counselling perspectives and orientations, and integrates these as and when it is appropriate in their practice. This is not to suggest that integrative counselling sessions resemble a 'lucky dip' activity, whereby the counsellor meets their client for the first time, closes their eyes, reaches into a bag and pulls out 'An Approach' – 'solution focused' or 'cognitive behavioural', for example – that is then adopted in counselling! Similarly, the term integration does not refer to a 'pick and mix' philosophy where the counsellor tries a 'little bit of this and a little bit of that' until something seems to help.

Like other counselling orientations, first and foremost the integrative counsellor recognises the value of the counselling relationship and their primary responsibility is to build this therapeutic alliance with their clients (Bordin, 1979; Green, 2010), in order that they can encourage the young person to begin to trust them enough to open up and 'tell their story'. It is through reflecting on the story with the young person that the counsellor is then able to use their professional judgement, in order to assess each client's needs and consider which counselling perspectives may be integrated usefully.

McLeod (2009) explains that the concept of integration developed originally in the 1960s and 1970s as a response to increasing numbers of practitioners who felt that no single counselling model was sufficient in a 'stand-alone' capacity, but that different models and approaches could be applied usefully as appropriate. In our experience as both counsellors and counsellor educators, it would be true to say that, when asked, most counsellors would suggest that they do not adhere rigidly to a single approach, but draw from their understanding of a range of counselling orientations to support their work with clients. O'Brien and Houston concur:

> Experiments show, for example, that when senior practitioners' work with clients is recorded, it is not possible to tell what theoretical base each one

is working from. It looks as if they are responding to the immediacy of the person in front of them.

(2000, p19)

Schön (1983) refers to this as the 'artistry of practice'.

Claringbull summarises the argument for integration neatly. He suggests that:

Integrative practitioners are free to import, mix and re-mix and generally fiddle about with, any elements from any of the entire range of available therapies as circumstances appear to indicate. For an increasing number of counsellors, integrative psychotherapy is emerging as the treatment method that seems to offer the most help to the most clients in most situations.

(2010, p112)

Of course, there are those who oppose this view (Eysenk, 1970; Szasz, 1978; Kennedy and Charles, 2002). Arguments against integration are likely to include concerns about counsellors having 'bits and pieces' of knowledge about different theoretical orientations which are limited and do not represent a full understanding. There are also concerns expressed that some of the approaches stem from very different philosophical and psychological standpoints. Lazarus (1995) suggests that integration should be approached with caution, as attempting to draw from concepts and ideologies that are fundamentally opposed might lead to unhelpful or negative interventions with clients. But it is important to note that the argument for integration has grown in strength in recent years. Evidence of its acceptance as an approach in its own right is clear to see, with a significant rise in the number of training courses available for integrative counselling.

Furthermore, it is, it could be argued, particularly pertinent to be prepared to be flexible in one's approach when working with young people. The counsellor who attempts to use a single model in their practice (be it psychodynamic, person-centred, cognitive behavioural, or others) may find that their young client experiences difficulty in responding or engaging fully in the process. Geldard and Geldard explain:

Adolescents are not children and they are not adults: they are in transition. We therefore need to tailor our counselling approaches to engage the adolescent directly and actively and to use strategies which will specifically address their needs in ways which are acceptable to them.

(2004, p57)

So far we have established some arguments for and against integration, and we are beginning to develop our understanding of what the approach is and what it is not. This is a helpful starting point, but what would be of value now is to begin to develop our understanding of what an integrative approach is in some detail and consider how it might be applied to counselling practice with young people. If an integrative approach is not a 'purist' approach, underpinned by a single set of 'rules', then what is it? What does it look like? If asked, how would we know that we were observing an integrative counsellor in action? Below, Janet, an integrative counsellor working in a voluntary counselling service for young people, explains her understanding and use of an integrative approach in her counselling work with adolescents.

Practitioner reflections: A counsellor's perspective – Janet

I suppose that I see myself as someone who, first and foremost, works to establish relationships of trust with young people. I guess that this is the most important thing in my work. I treat my clients with respect and, most importantly, I take them seriously. For some young people this may be the first time in their lives that they have been shown respect by an adult and have been listened to and not judged. That is important. And it can take time.

I help my clients to tell me why they have come for counselling. Sometimes they have been referred; someone else has said that they should have counselling and they are not sure why themselves. On other occasions, they have contacted the agency directly. Always, in early sessions, we spend time trying to get to the bottom of 'why counselling?' and 'why now?' and 'what do we want to achieve?'

I guess that my approach depends on what the presenting problem or issue is that the young person is bringing. For example, I might use solution-focused techniques for a client who is identifying a clearly defined problem, say an issue with time management if they are behind with their school work. Whereas for an issue such as bereavement or loss, I would take a more person-centred approach to 'being with' the person in their pain. Alternatively, if, for example, I'm working with a young person who has behavioural issues – panic attacks for instance, or self-harming – I might consider using cognitive behavioural techniques as part of the counselling.

Like I said before, my approach is basically focused on engaging with the young person and forming a relationship of trust, but within that, I feel free to select from a range of counselling approaches and techniques based on an assessment of their needs. I'm not rigid in my approach either. I think flexibility is important, but at the same time the counselling sessions are structured and purposeful. I guess there are times when I might get it wrong. That's when supervision comes in and helps me to reflect on what I've done and how I can alter my approach if necessary.

Janet explains the significance she attaches to forming a relationship of trust and openness with each young person she sees. She goes on to explain that it is important to establish the key issues or 'presenting problem' that each client is bringing to counselling. From an analysis of the client's needs, Janet selects a particular theoretical concept or technique to use. This is far from the 'pick and mix' approach mentioned earlier, but neither is it a purist or rigid description of a counselling orientation.

So, to summarise, the key principles of the integrative approach are as follows:

- all counselling approaches are valued;
- building a therapeutic alliance is paramount;
- assessment of needs is central;
- selection of appropriate techniques/concepts to integrate is key;
- working within a model that provides a structure for integration is important.

ACTIVITY 2.1

- What have you understood an integrative approach to mean thus far?
- To what extent does the discussion mirror your understanding of, and approach to, counselling young people?
- What do you see as the strengths of the approach for counselling young people?
- And the potential weaknesses?

A MODEL FOR INTEGRATION

In the description of her work above, Janet suggests that she takes a 'structured and purposeful' approach to her counselling with young people and this is important. Those who have been trained as integrative counsellors are likely to have been introduced to a particular model, which provides this 'structured approach' to integration. An example of this kind of framework is Egan's three stage model (2007). There are other integrative models (Clarkson, 2003; Culley and Bond, 2004; Geldard and Geldard, 2004; Evans and Gilbert, 2005) but as Egan's work is widely recognised internationally and his 'skilled helper' approach to 'helping relationships' is used across a range of counselling contexts (for example, couple counselling, personal counselling, career counselling, mental health counselling, and others) it is worthy of further exploration here.

Egan's three stage model was originally developed in the 1970s. It came about as a response to those who worked in a range of helping contexts, by suggesting a way to support 'helpers' in engaging in meaningful conversations with their clients. Jenkins (2000) explains that Egan developed his ideas in order to offer a practical model to those who are engaged in counselling relationships. The purpose of the model was not to provide a new orientation to practice or an alternative psychological or philosophical perspective, but rather to offer a practical, easily accessible framework for counsellors to work within. Egan's model does not align itself with a particular counselling orientation (although Egan stresses the importance of adhering to person-centred core conditions in practice); neither does it exclude any complementary approach to counselling. What the model does is to offer counsellors a flexible but structured approach to their interactions, in which they can integrate or subsume other counselling perspectives (Woskett, 2006). The model also reflects a recognised pattern of decision making for clients. Egan explains the philosophy at the core of his approach to helping:

> *Helpers are successful to the degree to which their clients – through client-helper interactions – are better positioned to manage specific problem situations and develop specific unused resources and missed opportunities more effectively. Notice that this stops short of saying that clients actually end up managing problems and developing opportunities better. Although counsellors help clients achieve valued outcomes, they do not control those lives directly. In the end, clients can choose to live more effectively or not.*
>
> (2002, p7)

Egan is referring here to the fundamental need to value and respect clients, recognising that it is the client, not the counsellor, who is responsible for decision making about their lives (this draws from person-centred/humanistic principles discussed in detail in Chapter 3). It is also important to note that the model is grounded in the key counselling skills which ensure that a purposeful helping relationship is established. Without an atmosphere of respect or the appropriate use of a range of key skills (Culley and Bond, 2004), effective counselling may be compromised.

In brief, each stage of the model should focus on the following:

Stage one – 'What's going on?'

- Establishing a relationship of openness and trust.
- Enabling the client to 'tell their story'.
- Establishing the nature, breadth and depth of the issues raised.
- Agreeing the focus or agenda for counselling.
- Sharing expectations about what can be achieved.

Stage two – 'What solutions make sense for me?'

- Exploring issues in depth.
- Focusing on feelings and behaviour.
- Challenging perceptions and re-framing where appropriate.
- Considering and evaluating options for change.
- Identifying a 'preferred scenario'.
- Establishing possible barriers to change.
- Identifying strategies to overcome barriers to change.

Stage three – 'How do I get what I need or want?'

- Identifying possible action steps.
- Evaluating the pros and cons of action.
- Planning specific SMART (specific, measureable, achievable, realistic, time-bound) action steps.
- Setting timescales for action.

It could be argued that the model appears to be prescriptive and inflexible. But it is not designed to be used in a formulaic and linear way. Indeed, Egan stresses the need for flexibility. In counselling relationships it is unlikely that each stage will be worked through in one interaction (in fact, it would be very surprising if it was). It may well be that it takes a number of sessions to establish a relationship of trust between the counsellor and client in order to enable the young person to tell their story (stage one). Furthermore, the 'story' may change, the emphasis may alter and other issues not initially recognised as important may become paramount as the story unravels. Often young people's lives are both chaotic and fast-moving, and there is a need for counsellors to be mindful of that and to use the model flexibly in their work, renegotiating as appropriate. This is illustrated in the case study below about **Stuart**, **Nashreen** and **Olga** who are at stage one of Egan's model.

Case study 2.1   Young people in counselling: stage one of Egan's model

Stuart, aged 15, has seen his counsellor for three sessions. During the first session he was reluctant to engage, did not make eye contact and resisted any attempt by his counsellor to encourage him to speak about why he had come for counselling. He returned the following week for his second appointment (much to his counsellor's surprise) and on this occasion he responded to his counsellor, but in a limited way, giving little detail and continuing to appear uncomfortable. On the third session, however, Stuart began to open up. He made more eye contact and spoke in longer sentences about his situation. Stuart is in stage one of Egan's model. The relationship is still being established and the reasons for counselling have not yet been explored fully. Stuart is just beginning to trust the counsellor enough to 'tell his story'. The counsellor's concern at this stage is to focus on building a relationship, providing Stuart with the time and support he needs to help him to feel safe in counselling.

Nashreen, aged 17, arrived for her first session and 'spilled out' her situation to her counsellor. She explained that she is going through a tough time with her boyfriend. They've been together for two years, but they are always arguing and 'splitting up'. This is making her unhappy and she wants to work on understanding and changing this aspect of their relationship. At the end of the first session, Nashreen seems to have worked through stage one of Egan's model (what's going on?) and is ready to begin focusing on stage two (what solutions make sense for me?). Of course, it may be that in subsequent sessions other issues emerge which will require a reassessment of 'what's going on?'

Olga, aged 13, arrived for the first session with her counsellor. She had been referred to counselling as she self-harms. Olga was reluctant to engage at first, but begins to respond and reveals a life that is chaotic and deeply unhappy. The self-harming, for which she was originally referred, is just a small part of a much bigger picture. Several subsequent sessions are needed in order for Olga and her counsellor to establish the nature and depth of the issues she wants to work on and to prioritise an order for addressing these. Stage one takes six sessions, and the counsellor is mindful that new issues are likely to emerge that may mean revisiting stage one during subsequent sessions.

Geldard and Geldard (2004) emphasise the importance of this early stage of relationship building within an integrative approach to counselling young clients. They suggest that the focus on building an effective counselling relationship is paramount and that the humanistic core conditions (Rogers, 1951) of empathy, congruence and unconditional positive regard are central (see Chapter 3).

Once the relationship is developed and the counsellor has gathered together the threads of the young person's story and helped their client to identify and assess the key issues that they would like to work on in counselling, progress can be made to stage two ('what solutions make sense for me?'). At this stage, Egan emphasises the need to consider possibilities, evaluate the suitability of these possibilities, challenge clients to reflect on the implications of the options open to them, identify any 'blind spots' and move towards selecting the option or goal that the young person decides will work best for them. It is in stage two in particular that counsellors may consider and select other counselling approaches to integrate. In order to establish and build a therapeutic alliance, they are already adhering to person-centred core conditions of empathy, congruence and unconditional positive regard. Now, having assessed their client's needs in stage one, they are in a position to reflect on alternative therapeutic approaches that may be integrated as appropriate. For example, a client who has identified an issue of recurrent panic attacks (an unhelpful and limiting behaviour) as something they want to work on, may be helped by using cognitive behavioural techniques in stage two (see Chapter 6). Possible strategies for dealing with the attacks when they happen can be discussed, it is hoped, to minimise their impact. The integrative counsellor, using Egan's three stage model as a framework, has drawn on their knowledge of counselling approaches (in this example, cognitive behavioural approaches, which are recognised as being effective when clients bring limiting behavioural issues to counselling).

Let's return to **Stuart**, **Nashreen** and **Olga** in the examples outlined above and see how they are progressing through stage two of Egan's model.

Case study 2.2   Young people in counselling: stage two of Egan's
                  model

Stuart has now attended counselling for a total of 12 sessions. He has 'opened up' considerably and talked about his home life (he lives with his mum, who is an alcoholic, and two younger siblings). Stuart has also expressed feelings of isolation at school. His school attendance has suffered because he has to take his younger siblings to school and then he goes home without attending school himself. He often 'hangs out' with a group of young men who do not attend school either and he spends time with them smoking dope and listening to music. Now that a fuller picture of Stuart's story has emerged, he and his counsellor begin to explore what he would like to change in his life and how he is going to achieve this. The counsellor helps Stuart to understand his feelings about his situation, but also integrates solution-focused techniques (see Chapter 8) to help him to think about small, incremental changes that it is within his power to make. During stage two, Stuart's demeanour begins to alter and he takes a more proactive approach in his counselling sessions.

Nashreen has moved very swiftly to stage two ('what solutions make sense for me'?). She established in the first session that she wanted to talk about her relationship with her boyfriend – in particular, the cycle of arguments, splitting up and getting back together – which is 'getting her down'. In stage two, the counsellor uses aspects of transactional analysis (see Chapter 5) to encourage Nashreen to explore how she and her boyfriend interact and to identify the 'subtext' of their relationship. This exploration leads Nashreen to realise that she and her boyfriend are involved in a complex game whereby each 'acts out' certain roles in order to get what they want in the relationship, often at the other's expense. The counsellor encourages Nashreen to think about how she could respond differently in order to ensure that both she and her boyfriend make decisions that are acceptable to each other. However, what Nashreen has also divulged is that her parents disapprove of her relationship with her boyfriend and have banned her from seeing him (although she still does). Thus, the counsellor and Nashreen return to stage one to explore the issue of her parents' disapproval in more depth.

Olga has set out the complex and deep-rooted issues that are impacting on her life. Through an exploration of these in stage one it has become apparent that much of what Olga is experiencing stems from her lack of self-esteem and confidence, engendered primarily by experiences of abuse she suffered in childhood. In stage two, counselling focuses on helping Olga to reflect on and understand her feelings more clearly, to stop blaming herself for what happened to her as a young child and to start to see herself in a different way. The counsellor continues to work within the core conditions of the person-centred approach, showing empathy, congruence and unconditional positive regard at all times. In addition, the counsellor also integrates 'reframing' techniques from their under-standing of cognitive behavioural approaches (see Chapter 6). These reframing strategies enable Olga to begin to see her situation differently and to recognise her strengths, rather than dwell on her weaknesses.

COMMENT

In each of the cases above, the counsellor has used knowledge of other counselling approaches, integrated as appropriate, in order to enable the client to explore their situation in more depth, to consider what a 'preferred scenario' might look like and how issues might be resolved. Once clients have established the changes they want to make in their lives and thought through the consequences of their options, they are then in a position to turn their thoughts into action. This is where the counsellor assists the young person to move into stage three of the process. At this stage, the emphasis of counselling is on planning action – translating the goals that clients have spent time deciding on, into specific action in order that positive change can take place. Beware! There is a danger that some young people (and counsellors for that matter) will move to action before issues have been explored in sufficient depth and goals have been thought through and examined from every angle. Where this is the case, actions are unlikely to be carried out, barriers will continue to get in the way and clients may repeat previous patterns in their lives and admit defeat. Let's return to **Stuart**, **Nashreen** and **Olga** who are now in stage three of Egan's model.

Case study 2.3 Young people in counselling: stage three of Egan's model

Stuart has attended for 20 sessions in total. He is now at ease with his counsellor and appears to value his counselling appointments (always arriving on time and never missing a session). Stuart has decided on changes that he would like to make in his life (that are within his scope) and now he and his counsellor start to explore what needs to be done in practice. Stuart has identified the following goals:

- improve his school attendance;
- smoke less dope;
- spend less time 'hanging out' with his friends;
- encourage his mum to get some help with her drinking issues.

During stage three, Stuart's counsellor helps him to identify and evaluate various action steps associated with his goals, ensuring that a number of possibilities are considered carefully. The counsellor knows that it is important at this stage to ensure that any action steps are realistic and achievable. They are also aware of the importance of ensuring that the action is Stuart's action and not their own. They take time to help Stuart to reflect carefully on the barriers that might get in the way of the action being successful. Now, after 25 counselling sessions, Stuart has built up a relationship of trust with his counsellor, identified and explored the issues that are having a negative impact on his life, considered goals for the future and planned action steps in relation to these to ensure positive change takes place.

Nashreen's counselling, which at first appeared to focus on the relationship with her boyfriend, has developed into a much more complex story. Her counsellor revisited stage one when it emerged in stage two that Nashreen had some difficult issues with her parents (including the fact that they had forbidden her from seeing her boyfriend). The agenda was renegotiated and a number of new goals explored in stage two. Nashreen is now ready to consider specific action steps that she is able to take. Nashreen feels strongly that she can't be honest with her parents about her relationship with her boyfriend; neither does she want that relationship to end. Her counsellor has encouraged her to think about the implications of continuing to see her boyfriend in secret (although clearly it is not down to her counsellor to tell Nashreen what to do). Nashreen's action steps focus on trying to communicate in a different way with her boyfriend, but she has also thought through action that she could take should her parents find out about the relationship. After 12 sessions with her counsellor, Nashreen decides that counselling has given her the help she needs at this point in her life.

Olga has worked hard in counselling and has engaged with the reframing activities that have been worked through in stage two with great success. However, when it comes to putting her goals into action, Olga finds it very difficult. She sets various action steps but is unable to carry them out. It becomes clear that the inability to take action is starting to reinforce Olga's earlier feelings of failure and lack of self-worth. It quickly becomes apparent that there is more work to be done in stage two, before Olga is ready to move to stage three of Egan's model.

REFLECTION POINT

- How effectively does the integrative approach taken in the cases above meet the needs of the young people?
- What do you see as the strengths of the approach, having followed through the cases outlined and what might be the challenges in each case?
- What might you have done differently with Stuart, Nashreen and Olga?

As suggested earlier, Egan's is not the only integrative model. It is, however, one that lends itself particularly well to work with young people because of its practical application. It does not simply offer a theoretical perspective, but rather a structured approach to effective counselling practice with an emphasis on skilled helping.

THE INTEGRATIVE APPROACH IN PRACTICE

We have identified the key features of an integrative approach to counselling, reflecting on the pros and cons of 'not ruling out' any specific theoretical orientation that might inform our practice. We have also examined a specific helping model – Egan's three stage model – which enables the counsellor to ground their practice in person-centred core conditions and to integrate other approaches as appropriate. To illustrate and encourage further reflection on the integrative approach to counselling young clients, it is helpful to begin by looking at the example below, of **Claire**, a school counsellor working with young people from 11 to 18.

Case study 2.4   Using an integrative approach in practice

Claire works as a counsellor in a large, inner-city comprehensive school. Young people are referred to her by colleagues in the school (these could be teachers, classroom assistants, learning mentors, school nurse, and so on) and sometimes they refer themselves for counselling. Currently, Claire is working with eight students whose cases are outlined briefly below:

Sam – a 14-year-old who has been referred because he finds it difficult to control his anger. He is constantly involved in fights with other students and he is abusive to teachers and other members of staff.

Charelle – a 13-year-old young woman who has been referred by the school nurse as she has lost a significant amount of weight very quickly with no apparent physical health reasons.

Toni – a 16-year-old young woman who has been bereaved recently. Her mother died suddenly after a short illness.

Junior – a 15-year-old young man who is living with foster parents and repeatedly runs away.

Tariq – a 12-year-old who shows signs of being school-phobic.

Gemma – a 16-year-old who is feeling stressed by her forthcoming exams and suffers with panic attacks.

Zoe – a 13-year-old who has been taken into care and is desperately unhappy and finding it difficult to adjust.

Tom – a 12-year-old who has been bullied by other students and appears frightened and withdrawn.

REFLECTION POINT

- Why might an integrative approach be appropriate for Claire's work as a school counsellor?
- What types of behavioural, emotional or psychological issues is Claire engaging with in each case?

Claire has been trained as an integrative counsellor. This means that she is flexible about the theoretical approaches she draws on in her practice. She is open to working with each young person in a slightly different way, using her knowledge of a range of approaches to inform her decisions about which theoretical perspectives to integrate into her practice. It is the problem or issue that each client presents, which then forms the integrating concept (Jenkins, 2000). For example, some of the young people identified above (Sam, Charelle and Gemma, for instance) are displaying specific unhelpful and limiting *behaviours*. This might suggest to Claire that integrating *cognitive behavioural* techniques in her sessions with these young people might be helpful in addressing the behaviour and underlying causes for the behaviour (see cognitive behavioural approaches, Chapter 6). Alternatively, Toni, Zoe and Tom are experiencing *emotional and psychological* rather than behavioural difficulties and Claire pays particular attention to applying *person-centred skills* to enable these clients to reflect on their feelings and work through their emotional turmoil in their sessions (see person-centred counselling, Chapter 3).

CHAPTER SUMMARY

The purpose of this chapter was to introduce the concept of integrative counselling, examine the principles of an integrative approach, establish a model for integration and consider the application of an integrative approach to counselling in practice. As was suggested at the start of the chapter, integration is a relatively new counselling orientation and, as with any approach, it is not wholeheartedly welcomed. Counsellors who have been trained in a single theoretical approach may argue that the dangers perceived in integration outweigh the benefits. However, we would respond that the approach is sound and highly appropriate to work with young people, as long as the assessment of client's needs is thorough and informed by a clear understanding of a range of theoretical perspectives and their application to practice. Integrative counsellors should be able to explain clearly why they have selected a particular approach and ruled out another in each case (and supervision provides the obvious forum for this reflection to take place).

What follows in this book is an introduction to a range of established approaches to counselling, all of which, we would argue, can be integrated as appropriate in counselling practice. It is therefore helpful to engage with the remainder of the book with this in mind. In order to develop your understanding further, we would suggest returning to this chapter on integrative approaches and the reflective activities suggested.

ACTIVITY 2.2

- Take a moment to reflect on how you will approach your reading following this chapter. You might want to consider undertaking an activity at the end of each subsequent chapter, whereby you reflect on your own counselling practice and consider if/how/when/why you have integrated the approach outlined with your clients. If you haven't, when might you consider it?

SUGGESTED FURTHER READING

Clarkson, P (2003) *The Therapeutic Relationship,* 2nd edition. London: Whurr.

An excellent and in-depth text which provides a thorough grounding in integrative counselling practice.

Culley, S and Bond, T (2004) *Integrative Counselling Skills in Action.* London: Sage.

A practical and accessible text that focuses on the application of an integrative approach.

Egan, G (2007) *The Skilled Helper*, 8th edition. Pacific Grove: Brooks/Cole.

Egan's writing is engaging and the three stage model introduced in this chapter is explored in depth.

Evans, K and Gilbert, G (2005) *An Introduction to Integrative Psychotherapy.* Basingstoke: Palgrave Macmillan.

An accessible text that sets out clearly the intricacies of integrating approaches and provides a suggested model for practice.

Geldard, K and Geldard, D (2009) *Counselling Adolescents*, 3rd edition. London: Sage.

A very readable book focusing specifically on an integrative approach with young people. Again, a model for counselling is explored.

Palmer, S and Woolfe, R (2000) *Integrative and Eclectic Counselling and Psychotherapy.* London: Sage.

A useful book in which authors address some key issues for integrative counselling. Although written in 2000, it still has some pertinent points to make.

Wosket, V (2006) *Egan's Skilled Helper Model.* London: Routledge.

This text provides a great introduction to Egan's model and a detailed exploration of the contexts in which the model can be applied.

CHAPTER 3

Exploring person-centred principles and developing counselling skills

by Jane Westergaard

> ## CORE KNOWLEDGE
>
> By the end of this chapter you will have the opportunity to:
>
> * identify the key principles underpinning a person-centred approach to counselling young people;
> * understand the application of the core conditions to counselling practice with young people;
> * examine a range of counselling skills;
> * develop the use of key counselling skills in your own practice.

INTRODUCTION

Those who work in a range of counselling contexts, supporting young people with complex and in-depth needs, know that building effective relationships is central to achieving positive outcomes. Young people who seek support (or are referred for it) often present with chaotic lives, low self-esteem, a lack of trust in counselling and the 'helping professions' and a reluctance to engage with the 'establishment'. To work effectively, counsellors should possess the relevant knowledge and skills to engage young people and to build relationships of trust. This can take time.

As suggested in Chapter 2, it is the responsibility of the practitioner to draw on their knowledge and understanding of established approaches to counselling, which they can utilise in order to enable young people to work towards positive change in their lives. But at the heart of integrative counselling practice, regardless of the different theoretical models and techniques that might be applied, lies the counsellor's adherence to the core conditions of a person-centred approach (Rogers, 1967). The application of these core conditions, coupled with the belief that young people have within themselves the resources and capacity for change (although these may be deeply buried and rarely glimpsed in some cases), should, over time, lead to the establishment of a trusting relationship: a therapeutic alliance. In order to build this relationship of trust, counsellors working with young people will have developed key skills to engage with their clients and maintain empathic, yet purposeful relationships.

This chapter sets out to address the two areas outlined above. First, it focuses on the person-centred approach; its key features and application to counselling young people and second, the chapter explores a range of skills that counsellors should develop in order to establish and maintain therapeutic relationships with young people.

The skills examined in this chapter are:

- active listening;
- reflection;
- helpful questioning;
- summarising;
- challenging;
- immediacy.

As in all the chapters in this book, there are opportunities for reflection at significant points throughout, as well as case study examples to illustrate both the person-centred approach and the use of key counselling skills in action. In addition, further reading is suggested at the end of the chapter.

THE PERSON-CENTRED APPROACH

All approaches to counselling recognise the importance of the quality of the relationship between the counsellor and client. This 'therapeutic alliance' (Saltzman et al., 1976; Bordin, 1979; Orlinsky et al., 1994; Tudor et al., 2004) requires the counsellor to understand the uniqueness of their client and to ensure that they enter their client's frame of reference without imposing their own values, beliefs and behaviours. Prever sums this relationship up:

> *Despite all the important and valued interventions into the lives of young people in difficulty made by parents, family and professionals, it is, in my experience, very rare that a young person coming to counselling has ever experienced the kind of warmth, openness, acceptance and empathy which are characteristic of the person-centred way of working.*

> (2010, p12)

The person-centred approach developed by Rogers (1967), and grounded in humanistic and existential philosophy, places particular emphasis on the nature of the helping relationship. It is a fundamentally optimistic approach which recognises that every individual is unique, has inner resources to enable development, and is capable of taking responsibility for, and making decisions about, their lives. However, it also suggests that barriers, erected in response to others' acceptance or valuing, may prevent individuals from achieving their aspirations. These principles are set out in brief below:

- we are all unique;
- human nature is fundamentally 'good' and positive;
- we each possess the drive to self-actualise (to become who we want to become);
- we all need to be loved and valued by others;
- we are best placed to make decisions about our own lives.

REFLECTION POINT

- What is your personal response to these principles?
- How much do they hold true in your own life?

COMMENT

It is the role of the counsellor (regardless of theoretical orientation) to engage with their client by building a relationship of trust. In the person-centred approach (and, increasingly in many other counselling approaches) this relationship is grounded in a set of 'core conditions'. By valuing the principles of person-centred philosophy and adhering to these core conditions, counsellors will provide their clients with the opportunity to develop self-understanding and discover their inner resources and strengths, optimising their opportunity for self-actualisation.

Mearns and Thorne (2000) provide a useful definition of these six 'core conditions'.

1 Two people need to be in relational and psychological contact.
2 One of those people (the client) should be incongruent – anxious, uncertain, experiencing problems, issues or difficulties.
3 The other person (the counsellor) should be willing to engage in the relationship and to work for the best outcomes for the client.
4 The counsellor should demonstrate an empathic approach.
5 The counsellor should be congruent – genuine, self-aware, and open.
6 The counsellor should demonstrate unconditional positive regard – taking a non-judgemental approach, recognising the client's right to their own beliefs and values.

Those who counsel young people need to be aware of the significance of these conditions and of the importance of the last three in particular. As an adult engaged in a counselling relationship with a young person, feeling and demonstrating empathy, remaining congruent and demonstrating unconditional positive regard can be challenging, but are crucial in building a therapeutic alliance. The last three core conditions are explored in more detail below.

Empathy

Empathy is a word that is often used by those in helping relationships. This is because demonstrating an empathic response to clients is central to building a therapeutic alliance. Empathy means attending to the young person and working to understand how they are thinking, feeling and behaving. By attempting to understand the young person's frame of reference (rather than considering their situation from your own adult perspective), thus demonstrating empathy, counsellors will be taking early steps in building a relationship of trust. Only when the young person begins to feel safe, valued and understood in the relationship will they have the confidence to be open and honest about the issues they are facing. McLeod explains:

> *Rogers suggested that when the counsellor/helper is able to understand the client, and accurately convey that understanding, the person will become more able to accept previously denied or warded-off aspects of their own experience. In person-centred counselling, it is important to stay within the 'frame of reference' of the client, to 'walk in their shoes', to 'see the world the way they see it', and not to respond on the basis of your own projections, experiences or to offer advice.*

> (2004, p53)

It is important for counsellors to recognise the difference between empathy and sympathy as mistaking sympathy for empathy can be harmful. The case study outlined below clarifies this difference.

Case study 3.1   Sympathy or empathy?

James, a 14-year-old, has told his counsellor that his sister has recently been run over by a car and is in intensive care. At the same time his parents are going through a marriage break-up and have little time for James. James is desperately unhappy and has started to shoplift on a regular basis. Last week he was 'caught in the act' and now faces prosecution.

Sympathetic response
'Oh, you poor thing. I'm so sorry. How absolutely terrible for you. What can I do to help sort this mess out for you?'

Empathic response
'It sounds like so much is going on for you right now and things are really tough. I get the feeling, from the way you're talking about it, that this latest incident feels like the 'straw that broke the camel's back' and you're feeling desperate. Have I got that right?'

COMMENT

In the case study above, the empathic response does not try to 'take away' or minimise the situation for James. Neither does it pretend that everything can be 'sorted'. What it does, is recognise the desperate situation in which James finds himself and demonstrates that the counsellor is working hard to understand how James feels, rather than acting in a 'parent' role. Prever (2010) emphasises the importance of counsellor empathy and identifies three levels of empathic response:

- reflecting back meaning and understanding to the client;
- reflecting back feelings;
- demonstrating 'advanced empathy', a deeper understanding of what is being expressed.

The experienced counsellor has the ability to 'go beyond' simply recognising what has been said and to demonstrate understanding at a deeper, emotional level.

REFLECTION POINT

- Can you remember working with a client where you found it difficult to feel and demonstrate empathy? What got in the way?
- How did you 'manage' your struggle with being empathic? What impact did this have on the counselling?

Congruence

Like empathy, the core condition of congruence is central to a person-centred approach and it is important that counsellors are aware of the need to be congruent – or genuine – in their work with young people, to be fully engaged and to be 'themselves', rather than 'playing the role' of helper. Being congruent requires high levels of self-awareness. A counsellor must 'check out' their responses regularly, asking themselves how they are thinking and feeling about the young person with whom they are working.

Rogers (1967) explained that congruence is about ensuring that thoughts, feelings and expressions 'match up,' that the counsellor demonstrates that they are 'real' and 'involved'. This does not mean expressing all that you feel, as a counsellor. For example, it would not be helpful to say 'I don't know what it is about you, but you're really getting on my nerves!' to a young person who has just arrived for counselling. This is likely to be a damaging response and not helpful in any way apart from having pro-vided the counsellor with the opportunity to vent their feelings. However, sometimes expressing feelings to clients can be helpful. For example, 'when you talk about your relationship with your mum, I start to feel very sad,' is the counsellor's empathic and genuine response to their client. This congruent response is one that might be used in the counselling relationship in a positive way. It demonstrates advanced empathy and also gives the young person 'permission' to examine their own feelings about their relationship with their mother.

REFLECTION POINT

How would you manage your feelings in the following situations, while remaining congruent?

- You are counselling a young person who espouses racist views.
- You feel frightened by your client's aggressive responses in the counselling room.
- You are bored with a client who comes week after week but doesn't appear to be making any progress.
- You feel sexually attracted to your client.

COMMENT

There is no 'right' response to the question posed above, because being congruent means examining our own individual feelings and these will vary from person to person. It is important, though, to reflect on how voicing your own felt response might be helpful to *the client*. Expressing your own feelings of fear, for example (as in example two) might assist your client to reflect on the impact of their aggressive attitude in other situations in their lives. There may be times (particularly in the last example, above) where your own feelings should be aired in supervision (another relationship which parallels that between client and counsellor in which congruence is required).

Unconditional positive regard

In addition to empathy and congruence, counsellors should understand the importance of adopting the core condition of 'unconditional positive regard' in their work with young people. Put simply, this means that whatever a young person does or says, the counsellor's acceptance of them as a valued human being with the potential to progress is unconditional. This does not mean having to like all young people or agree with them, but it does mean having to accept their right to hold their own beliefs and values – and the rights of young people have increased in recent years. The core condition of unconditional positive regard is not a mantle to be put on and taken off at whim. Rather it is a way of being, something that is experienced rather than simply demonstrated (this applies to all the core conditions, of course). Wilkins (2001, p42) highlights how important it is to 'connect with the person behind the "repulsive" or "repugnant" behaviour or attitude'.

No one said that demonstrating unconditional positive regard (or any of the core conditions for that matter) is easy! It can be extremely difficult for counsellors to accept their clients regardless of the stories they tell and the choices they make in their lives. However, this is a core condition for a reason. Person-centred counsellors would argue that if these core conditions are adhered to over a period of time, then change *is possible*.

REFLECTION POINT

- Can you think of clients for whom you simply did not feel (and were unable to demonstrate) unconditional positive regard? What impact did this have on the counselling?
- How do you think the outcome might have been different if you were able to demonstrate unconditional positive regard?
- What might you do if you are aware that you are struggling to demonstrate unconditional positive regard with a young person?

Working within these core conditions is not straightforward and demands constant reflection. It can be too easy to see the 'label' attached to the young person by others, without focusing on the 'person at the centre' (this is explored in more detail in Chapter 4). When these core conditions underpin supportive relationships with young people, much can be achieved. But the approach does not offer a 'quick fix'. Change comes about over time as the young person begins to feel valued and understood, and develops the confidence to take responsibility for decisions and actions. For many counsellors working with young people (particularly those based in schools) time is likely to be at a premium and immediate action may need to be taken in response to a crisis in a young person's life. The core conditions will provide a sound base for the counsellor to integrate other approaches and strategies into their work (see Chapter 2).

SKILLS FOR EFFECTIVE HELPING

The person-centred approach is grounded in the core conditions outlined above. To enable the counsellor to engage effectively with the young person and demonstrate empathy, congruence and unconditional positive regard in their work, they will need to develop a range of counselling skills. This chapter moves on to examine six key counselling skills. Three of these can be described as 'foundation' skills as they form the bedrock of all communication. These skills are active listening, using reflection and helpful questioning. The remaining skills – summarising, challenging and using immediacy – are not general conversational skills, but are 'advanced skills' which are central to counselling relationships.

FOUNDATION SKILLS

Active listening

An essential element to any conversation is listening. However, listening in a conversation and active listening in a counselling relationship are two different concepts. The skill of active listening is the ability to listen deeper than the words. It is about 'listening' with all our senses, in particular our eyes, which will pick up the facial expressions of our clients; and our 'feel' for what the client is saying through their body language, tone of voice and non-verbal communication.

It is not simply the ability to listen that is important. The counsellor should *demonstrate* active listening by ensuring that their eye contact, body language, tone of voice and facial expressions reflect and respond accurately to what is being said. Eye contact should be consistent, but not intense, body posture should be open and relaxed, use of language should be clear, evenly paced and para-verbal responses such as 'hmm, aha, OK', should be used to encourage and affirm. It is important at this point to emphasise the need for raised awareness about cultural difference (see Chapter 4). It cannot be assumed that because a client is not making eye contact, they are shy or disinterested. It may be that the client's cultural background considers direct eye contact to be disrespectful. It is the responsibility of the helper to 'check out' and understand the client's cultural identity and behavioural influences and work with these appropriately (Bimrose, 1996).

The energy required to 'actively listen' should not be underestimated, and neither should its importance in relation to the effectiveness of the engagement and the building of a trusting, open relationship. At times counsellors, for a range of reasons often to do with client's desperate situations, find themselves compelled to move quickly from listening to taking action. Collander-Brown (2005) describes this as the imperative to Do Something Now (DSN). However, resisting this urge to act and continuing to focus on helping the young person to explore their thoughts and feelings by active listening, will demonstrate empathy and encourage them to 'own' their issues and to believe that they have the resources to effect change.

ACTIVITY 3.1

- Invite a friend or colleague to talk to you for a few minutes about something that is an issue in their lives (a problem that they do not mind sharing). Resist the urge to respond verbally to them (and resist the temptation to offer solutions), but listen actively with all your senses to what they have to say. Demonstrate this listening with appropriate body language, eye contact and para-verbal responses to indicate encouragement and understanding.
- After a few minutes, end the interaction and reflect back to your friend/colleague the key thoughts and feelings that you have heard.
- Ask your friend/colleague to feed back to what extent they felt listened to, understood and empathised with.

Often, being actively listened to by an adult will be a new experience for many young people and the power of listening in counselling should not be underestimated.

Using reflection

The skill of using reflection, or reflecting back, is an important aspect of active listening. It has already been alluded to above. Reflecting back is about the counsellor 'holding a mirror' to their client by ensuring that responses are appropriate and that they reflect accurately the words and feelings that the young person is expressing. Mearns and Cooper explain further:

> *Invitations to the client to explore their experiences more deeply can take many forms. At the most basic level, it may simply involve reflecting back to clients a word or phrase they have used.*

> (2005, p121)

Culley and Bond describe the skill of using reflection as 'restating'. They explain that:

Restating involves repeating back to clients either single words or short phrases which they have used. It is an efficient way of prompting further discussion.

(2004, p34)

The case study below shows **Julian**, the counsellor, actively listening to **Lloyd** and reflecting back key words or phrases to invite Lloyd to think about what he has said and what he is feeling in greater depth.

Case study 3.2   Listening and reflecting in counselling

Lloyd: 'I hate school. It pisses me off.' (silence)

Julian: 'So you *hate* school . . .'

Lloyd: 'Yeah.' (silence) 'Well, I hate the way that everyone is always on my case.'

Julian: 'You feel that *everyone* is giving you a hard time . . .'

Lloyd: 'Yeah.' (silence) 'Well, not everyone. It's alright seeing my mates and that. It's the teachers. They piss me off.'

Julian: 'So it's your teachers that give you a hard time . . .'

Lloyd: 'Yeah.' (silence) 'Well, not all of them. Mr Smith is OK and I like PE, but Mrs Jones pisses me off. She's always having a go at me about stuff. She picks on me. It's true. Ask anyone.'

COMMENT

In the case above, Lloyd moves from his first, very broad statement about 'hating school' to a place whereby he is starting to reflect on what specifically he finds challenging. Julian the counsellor has done nothing more than reflect back key words to Lloyd, enabling to him to 'hear' what he has said, reflect on it and re-establish his meaning. What should also be noted is that Julian reflects what Lloyd has said, but does not attempt to replicate Lloyd's use of language exactly. It is important that counsellors remain congruent (true to self) in the counselling relationship.

REFLECTION POINT

- How much do you use the skill of reflection in your own counselling practice?
- It can be helpful to record your counselling sessions (with the permission of the client, of course) and analyse the way you use your counselling skills, including the skill of reflection.

Helpful questioning

Listening and reflecting back are important, but to enable young people to explore in depth, counsellors will, at some point, need to ask questions. When asked, counsellors early in their training are likely to say that the reason for asking questions is in order to gain information about clients. This is, of course, correct, but it is by no means the only reason. The primary purpose of questioning is to invite clients to think in detail about their lives. It encourages reflection, analysis and evaluation, invites clients to 'think through' their ideas and feelings, and establishes the nature and depth of the issues which they are facing.

The questions that offer a best 'fit' for helping interactions are *open* questions. These are characterised by the need for more than a 'yes', 'no', or 'don't know' response. For example, asking a young person 'how did you feel about that?' will invite deeper thinking than asking a *closed* question like 'did you enjoy it?' Open questions usually start with 'how', 'when', 'what', 'why', or 'tell me about'. Questions such as these will encourage reflection and young people should not be hurried to answer. The impetus to 'rescue' a young person who appears to be struggling to respond should be resisted. By hurrying a response or providing one of their own, the counsellor is effectively saying 'let me do this for you. What I think is . . .' and the relationship ceases to be person-centred. Initially, for some young people an open question like 'how do you feel?' can seem overwhelming. If this is the case, the counsellor can begin with a closed question, for example, 'have you been excluded from school?' and then follow it up with an open question such as 'what happened?'

Experienced counsellors will have discovered the value of asking *hypothetical* questions. Otherwise referred to as 'what if?' questions, these are helpful in encouraging young people to consider consequences and evaluate options without personalising and risking a defensive response. For example, counsellor: 'Let's imagine that you tell your mum that you want to move away from home and live with your boyfriend. How might she react?' The school counsellor (in this case) is setting up a hypothetical scenario which can be examined more objectively; providing the young person with the opportunity to distance themselves from the immediate situation, while at the same time giving consideration to what their options are and the consequences of the actions they might be tempted to take. Culley and Bond support the view that:

> *Hypothetical questions are useful for helping clients to articulate their fears and explore them in the relative safety of the helping relationship.*
>
> (2004, p43)

Sometimes counsellors can be quick to label their clients 'quiet', 'disinterested' or 'withdrawn' when in fact it is their own use of questioning skills that have not provided the opportunity for clients to think, feel and speak. A relentless list of closed questions (will you, did you, can you, are you?) is likely to encourage an atmosphere that resembles an interrogation rather than a helping interaction. Questioning is a conversational skill that we use every day with our friends, families, colleagues and others. However, that does not mean that when used in helping relationships it is straightforward. Like active listening, much thought needs to be given to how questions are used, at what point they should be asked and what should be said, in order to enable greater depth of reflection and understanding.

ACTIVITY 3.2

Have a go at practising your use of open and hypothetical questions.

- Work with a friend or colleague (you could use the same scenario you worked on earlier in the 'active listening' activity) and use open and hypothetical questions to encourage your friend/colleague to explore the issues they are facing further.
- Ask your friend to respond 'yes/no' if asked a closed question, thus closing the interaction down.

ADVANCED SKILLS

Summarising

The skill of summarising is not a common conversational skill. A summary involves the helper in actively listening to the young person and then paraphrasing the key ideas, thoughts and feelings in condensed form. In brief, summaries are used to:

- confirm that active listening has taken place;
- demonstrate empathy;
- clarify understanding;
- invite the young person to reflect;
- keep the interaction structured, shared and focused;
- encourage a relationship of trust;
- highlight themes or tensions;
- agree action points.

For the reasons outlined above, it is important that the skill of summarising is used throughout the interaction, not just at the conclusion, as its name might imply. In particular, it is helpful at the end of each stage of the process (see Egan's (2007) three stage model in Chapter 2) in order to agree what has been discussed and signpost a way forward.

Summarising takes practice. It needs to be used sensitively and should take place as a congruent, organic response rather than a contrived one. Even though it may feel mechanistic to begin with, practice will ensure summaries become reflective rather than merely repetitive. Counsellors will develop a sense for when to summarise. It requires intuition and can only be effective in response to active listening. In the case study below, **Meena**, a teenage pregnancy counsellor uses the skill of summarising with her client, **Anna**.

Case study 3.3   Summarising in practice

Meena: *It sounds as though you have really thought through the implications of going ahead with your pregnancy, Anna. You've talked things through with the baby's father and with your parents and you sound really relieved to have done that. You seem to feel very happy and excited about the pregnancy today. It all feels quite different from how you were last time we met. How does that sound to you?*

By summarising what she has heard (words, thoughts and emotions) Meena is demonstrating empathy and understanding. Anna has the opportunity to reflect on what she has said, check it out for accuracy and explore her situation further.

Sometimes, counsellors in training are concerned that over-use of the skill of summarising can seem patronising to the young person. Repeated attempts to interject with 'so, what you are saying is . . .' might seem unhelpful and clumsy. In fact, the reverse is true. Clients, when asked, report back that it has been really helpful to know that their counsellor is listening and understands how they feel. They explain that it also gives them the opportunity to 'listen back', reflect on what they have said and to correct any misunderstandings that have arisen.

REFLECTION POINT

- How much do you use the skill of summarising in your own counselling practice? How useful have you found it?
- It can be helpful to encourage clients to summarise for themselves at key points during the counselling. Try asking, 'so, where do you think we have got to? What are the main issues we've covered?' It can be enlightening to find that the client's perception of the 'main issues' might be at variance with your own.

Challenging

Challenging, like the skill of summarising, is not a natural conversational skill. It is used in counselling when:

- there is a discrepancy between words, thoughts and actions;
- consequences need to be thought through;
- realism is an issue.

When challenging, counsellors are enabling young people to be honest with themselves about their actions, the consequences of these actions and the need to be realistic about what can be achieved. Although counsellors accept that challenging is a 'good thing', and that the core conditions remain firmly in place, there is often a reluctance to challenge in counselling. There are two key reasons for this. First, it may be that the counsellor has not understood the principles of a person-centred approach fully. They may feel that to challenge is to go against a person-centred philosophy. In fact, the reverse is true. Being person-centred is about investing fully in the helping relationship in order to enable personal growth and greater understanding. Challenging is often the means by which this understanding can be gained. Second, there may be a fear that the challenge will appear confrontational and the client will defend against it and withdraw from the relationship. This is a risk, and emphasises the need for counsellors to be skilful in their challenges. If they are both sensitive and tentative in their approach, then the challenge will be accepted for what it is – a helpful intervention.

So, how are challenges used effectively? Challenging in itself is not a single skill, but is a composite of other key helping skills.

- **Active listening** – facial expressions and tone of voice can often be all that is needed to challenge. A raised eyebrow or a questioning smile can suggest 'what you have just said contradicts something you said earlier. Let's explore that a bit more.'
- **Helpful questioning** – in particular, hypothetical questions can be used to challenge a young person to think through the consequences of their actions and to be realistic about their decisions. 'Let's just imagine that . . . how might you respond?'
- **Summarising** – if there are discrepancies in what the young person is saying during the interaction, it can be helpful to challenge these by using the client's own words to highlight the discrepancy. For example, 'Earlier you said something about feeling ignored by your friends and left out of things that are going on. What you are saying now is that you are planning a weekend away with your friends soon to Spain. I'm wondering about this conflicting picture . . .?'

Although challenging is a supportive and positive activity, it does come with a 'health warning'. Challenging too early in counselling, before rapport has been established and trust has been gained, can be risky. However sensitively the challenge is made, the right to make it needs to be earned. It is important that the counsellor is clear about why they are challenging the young person and what they expect the challenge to achieve. A clumsy challenge that does not appear to be relevant to the issues under discussion is likely to harm the relationship that has been built. Culley and Bond (2004) suggest guidelines for using the skill of challenge.

- Be tentative not confrontational. Use language that conveys a 'hunch' or a 'feeling' rather than a fact when you challenge.
- Keep the aims of the challenge in mind. Remember that challenge is all about helping clients to explore and reassess, not about telling young people what to do.
- Make sure that the client is able to 'hear' and understand the challenge. Clients in a highly emotional or vulnerable state may not be resilient enough to accept a challenge for what it is – a helpful and positive intervention – but may defend against it or reject the challenger.
- Keep the challenge close to the client's perspective. Do not offer something as a challenge that is alien to the young person's understanding. Find a different way of posing the challenge that makes sense to the client.
- Be concrete and specific. Make clear to the young person exactly what the challenge refers to. This does not contradict the earlier suggestion of 'being tentative', but rather focuses on the need to be clear and unambiguous when it comes to challenging.
- Avoid finding fault or blaming. Always challenge from a 'no-blame' position. Blaming leads to defensiveness and is contrary to the core conditions of a person-centred approach.
- Encourage self-challenge. The most effective challenges are those that young people pose for themselves. The use of the skill of summarising can help clients to self-challenge.
- Be open to challenge. A counsellor who is defensive about their approach to counselling and unable or unwilling to hear a client's challenge is not well placed to encourage young people to accept challenges themselves.

ACTIVITY 3.3

Think about a client you have worked with recently for whom the skill of challenging was required.

- Why was the challenge required?
- How effectively did you challenge (what did you actually say/do)?

- How did the client respond to the challenge (in the room and subsequently)?
- How, if at all, might you have challenged more effectively?

Using immediacy

Using the skill of immediacy is closely allied to that of challenging. In fact immediacy, embedded in the core conditions of empathy, congruence and unconditional positive regard, can be used effectively as a challenge. Simply put, immediacy is a skill which is rooted firmly in the 'here and now' (Sutton and Stewart, 2002) and focuses on what is happening in the counselling room. It is a response by the counsellor to heightened emotions or tensions that have emerged. Culley and Bond explain:

Clients may not be aware of how they are feeling 'right now'. They may gain new awareness by staying with and exploring their thoughts and feelings as they occur 'now' in relation to you and to what they are revealing.

(2004, p129)

The example below shows **Chris**, a counsellor in the Child and Adolescent Mental Health Service (CAMHS), using immediacy with his client **Ben**, a 15-year-old who habitually starts fires.

Case study 3.4   Immediacy in action

Chris: 'So this most recent episode took place last week?'
Ben: 'Yeah.'
Chris: 'Tell me a bit about what happened.'
Ben: 'You know what happened. I started a fire on the heath. I've told you that already. What else do you want me to say? There's nothing more to say about it.'
Chris: 'Yes, you have told me what happened, but what we haven't talked about is how you're feeling now about what happened.'
Ben (defiantly): 'I feel fine about it. OK?'
Chris: 'I wonder why I'm getting the feeling that although you say you feel fine about what happened, there is actually something else going on here, Ben, and you really don't feel fine at all.'
Ben: 'Don't I?' (silence) 'Well how would you feel if your mum had a boyfriend half her age and was rubbing your nose in it? (angrily) You wouldn't feel "fine" then either, would you?'

COMMENT

In this case study, Chris has used the skill of immediacy to focus on the 'here and now'. He has developed an empathic understanding of Ben during counselling and he has picked up signals from Ben that although he is saying 'all is fine', everything about his response suggests that the opposite is true. Using immediacy enables Ben to own and explore how he is really feeling and the underlying causes of his emotional state. There are a number of reasons for using immediacy in counselling. They are as follows:

- when there is a perceived heightened emotional response that is unspoken in the room – 'I get the feeling that you are very sad today';
- when the young person is projecting feelings onto the counsellor – 'I wonder if you are worried that I'm going to tell you to 'get lost' like your dad did?';
- when there are perceived tensions in the counselling relationship – 'I get the sense that you are feeling quite angry about what I've just said';
- when immediate feedback is required – 'I just want to stop for a moment and tell you how brilliantly I think you are dealing with this.'

Immediacy is an advanced skill and, like challenge, should be offered tentatively. Counsellors in training (and those in practice too) often feel anxious about using immediacy. It requires advanced empathy and a certain amount of 'risk-taking' on the part of the counsellor who is, unusually perhaps, bringing themselves into the counselling. Notice in the examples above the use of 'I', spoken by the counsellor. Generally, in counselling, the counsellor's focus and attention is on the young person and enabling them to express *their* thoughts and feelings; the use of immediacy is different as it involves the counsellor directly. Where the core conditions are firmly in place and a therapeutic alliance has been established, immediacy can offer significant insight and can 'unblock' and help clients to move to greater understanding.

REFLECTION POINT

- Think about a client who you have worked with recently. Were there times that you might have used immediacy, but didn't? What stopped you?
- If you had used immediacy, what would you have said and how might the client have responded? How might this have been helpful?

CHAPTER SUMMARY

This chapter establishes the principles of a person-centred approach. It explains that positive change can occur when empathy, congruence and unconditional positive regard are demonstrated in the counselling relationships. It suggests that these core conditions are central to a range of counselling approaches, acting as a sound foundation on which other approaches and techniques may be built (see Chapter 2).

The skills examined in this chapter, used alongside the core conditions, are fundamental to building effective and purposeful relationships. The skills require practice and reflection to master. In the early days of counsellor training the development of these key skills may feel mechanistic and stilted, as each intervention is analysed and reflected upon. Over time, as the counsellor gains in experience and confidence, the use of counselling skills will become a natural and organic process. That said, even experienced counsellors should take time to reflect on their practice and their use of skills. As suggested before, supervision provides an opportunity to do just that.

SUGGESTED FURTHER READING

The texts below offer an excellent introduction to both the person-centred approach and to counselling skills:

Culley, S and Bond, T (2004) *Integrative Counselling Skills in Action.* London: Sage.

This is an extremely engaging book which examines how counselling skills are used in practice.

McLeod, J (2007) *Counselling Skill.* Berkshire: Open University Press

This is a very accessible book that sets out key skills and approaches for effective counselling. Chapter 8 is particularly useful.

Mearns, D and Thorne, B (1999) *Person-Centred Counselling in Action,* 2nd edition. London: Sage

This remains a core text which provides essential reading for person-centred counsellors.

Reid, HL and Fielding, AJ (2007) *Providing Support to Young People: A Guide to Interviewing in Helping Relationships.* London: RoutledgeFalmer.

A practical and engaging book for those who work with young people in a range of helping contexts.

Prever, M (2010) *Counselling and Supporting Children and Young People: A Person-Centred Approach.* London: Sage.

An excellent and very readable introduction to person-centred work with young people.

CHAPTER 4

Embedding multicultural principles and skills into counselling work with young people

by Hazel Reid

CORE KNOWLEDGE

By the end of this chapter you will have the opportunity to:

- clarify the term multiculturalism;
- explain the concepts of equal opportunity, social justice and anti-oppressive practice;
- consider a range of social variables, linked to social and economic context, culture and history;
- outline principles to increase multicultural awareness and effective practice;
- extend a multicultural vision through reflexive practice.

INTRODUCTION

A reflective practitioner recognises a need for continuous professional and personal development beyond their initial training and may discuss such needs in supervision. It is our view that the work of understanding how to interact with and counsel young people from diverse backgrounds is never complete. When a young person says, 'I don't know' they probably mean, 'I don't trust you enough to tell you.' This chapter explores what might get in the way of developing such trust.

Social justice is inherent within policies related to inclusion. Indeed, inclusion is viewed in many countries as the vehicle for integrating 'problem' youth and achieving social cohesion. In relation to the labelling of young people as problematic, the chapter challenges this by drawing on the 'externalising' statement of the late Michael White (1989, p7): 'The person is not the problem; the problem is the problem.' An exploration of cultural relations is also undertaken, alongside suggesting what the counsellor can do, in order to increase their multicultural awareness and effectiveness.

The chapter also relates the underlying philosophy of multiculturalism to individual action, by exploring the need for self-awareness as a prerequisite for 'awareness of others'. Principles that can be integrated into counselling with young people are identified with suggestions on how these may be incorporated within practice. In addition, through posing a number of reflexive questions, ideas for extending the counsellor's multicultural vision are included in an effort to promote social justice further.

WHAT IS MEANT BY MULTICULTURALISM?

The term can be viewed negatively and has been the subject of criticism in recent times, caused in part by the radicalism of some cultural groups and the global fear of terrorist attacks. As a result, liberal approaches to immigration have been questioned, and social and cultural division and tension in some sections of society has increased. This division is complex and should not be viewed as a simplistic 'black versus white' or the reverse – the tension is often between new and established groups regardless of colour. But, when the 'West' comes under threat, old stereotypical views of 'other' cultures re-emerge; as the perceived superiority of Western values and dominant beliefs leads to a view that 'other' civilisations are not really civilised at all (Parker, 2007). Clearly, there are issues related to power here and any theoretical model which aims to explain cultural difference needs to be examined to identify the social, cultural, historical and gendered assumptions that underpin its approach. At the individual level we will be attracted to explanations that fit with our own view of the world, that uphold the beliefs and values we have grown up with. Ian Parker, a critical psychologist, sums this up nicely, indicating how our attempts to understand 'difference' can cause further marginalisation:

> What we think we know about ourselves is bound up with culture, and it is always from a position in culture that we reflect on what makes us different from others. However, cultural differences in views about human psychology do not simply float around together, jostling up against each other to provide a richer multicultural dish. Psychology is not the melting pot or the tossed salad of academic research but the sorting machine that selects and grades people according to categories that most times are worse than useless, and often a little tasteless.
>
> (Parker, 2007, p36)

ACTIVITY 4.1

- Think about your name, your place of birth, your background and your cultural history – what story would you tell about yourself? Make brief notes on that story.

- How does the story you tell about yourself fit with what a colleague or friend would say about you? Find an opportunity to ask them and reflect on both versions, thinking about any assumptions made and how they might have arisen.

Multiculturalism, as used in this chapter, should not be confused with a liberal assimilation project that aims to create 'insiders' out of 'outsiders' by integrating them into the receiving society. A critical interpretation takes issue with a pluralist view that suggests that 'anyone can make it', given the right opportunities (Reid, 2005). For example, well-intentioned educational activities based on the culture of a particular ethnic minority group can be engaging, but are unlikely to redress the effects of years of oppression (Kincheloe and Steinberg, 1997).

While colour, religion and race are highly significant, the term multiculturalism as used in the counselling literature is not an exclusive discussion of the impact of these particular social variables. A multicultural approach seeks to develop an awareness of the potential impact of *any* social difference (for example, age, gender, social class, sexuality, ability or disability, and so on).

This too can be dangerous unless we move beyond biological and 'common sense' explanations with regard to difference. That said, it is important to acknowledge that 'race' is a social construct that many would consider transcends other social variables because of its visibility. Racism and views about the appropriateness of government and institutional responses to the effects of racism cannot be overemphasised (Parsons, 2009). Yet others may view social class (Roberts, 2005) as the single biggest influence in terms of young people's access to goods and services (including counselling) and the ability to make a 'real' choice about present action and future plans.

Not surprisingly, categorisation segregates and separates, and can reinforce difference, suggesting that if you fix the individual you can fix the problems in a society. In this way, by maintaining their separateness and subordination, the voices of marginalised groups can be suppressed, even where they may form the majority, either in a geographical location or as part of the population (for example, neither women nor young people are a minority group). On the other hand, while acknowledging that labelling individuals has negative effects, refusing to discuss the needs of particular groups for fear of labelling them can undermine the collective experience of people who are marginalised and serves to conceal unequal power relationships.

REFLECTION POINT

- Think about the cultural groups (based on gender, ethnicity, age, social class, disability, sexuality, additional needs and so on) that you work or study with. Ask yourself, what are the consequences of using those group labels for the individuals you work/interact with and for your practice?
- What are your expectations with regard to how different groups present their 'problems' in counselling (e.g. black and minority ethnic, gay, additional needs, unemployed, young offenders, looked after children or those labelled 'abused', 'depressed' 'addict' and so on). Where do those expectations come from, and how might they influence your practice?

POWER AND AGENCY

The 'authority' to label others is vested in those who have the power to organise and distribute resources in a society (Foucault, 1980). Space is limited here for an in-depth discussion (for a detailed study, see Besley, 2002), but it is important that the wider social processes that are at work in any community are considered beyond the obvious day-to-day preoccupations and constraints that we navigate in any counselling role. In counselling young people it is essential to question the agenda within which that work takes place. So, although we cannot dismiss the notion that young people do have individual agency and can access the power to change their life circumstances (and therefore may not fit into a group category), taking a position that ignores the social and economic context can be disempowering for the young people that we seek to support.

Nevertheless, the views of a white, middle-aged woman, living in Sussex and writing about such issues, can be questioned as not grounded in experience. For example, the historical identity of many people of colour has been told through a European colonising 'gaze': can the writer step aside from the relatively privileged world that an academic inhabits? Well no, but even though not qualified to speak from experience, a contribution to the conversation can be made, with the hope this opens up the possibility that in doing so anti-oppressive practice (Thompson, 1993) can be promoted. My own reflexivity, apparent in the previous statement, is a practice necessity when developing self-awareness in order to meet multicultural principles. Practice that oppresses (literally to keep in a subservient position – to weigh down) is often unconscious and can occur when we are not thinking about our own social and 'powerful' position.

With regard to this point, it can be argued that agencies providing counselling should match the profiles of their counsellors to the profiles of their clients; in other words, a black, Muslim counsellor for a black, Muslim client or a match based on age or gender, and so on. This can help to balance an ethnocentric approach based on dominant white, Western (and often male) values, which have their foundations in notions of 'normality' that are irrelevant to the client. As there is no single concept of what is 'normal', a starting point in any counselling relationship is to take account of 'difference' on *both* sides of the relationship, and be willing to talk about cultural issues at the start of the process. What is important here is to take account of the client's views and work to their preferences, rather than making stereotypical decisions about what will work best for certain groups. It needs to be acknowledged that profile matching, however desirable, can be difficult when resources, in terms of both funding and personnel, are limited. That said, this is an economic argument that ignores the greater effectiveness that can be derived from providing a diversity of provision to meet diverse needs. McLeod notes (1998, p180) 'there is plentiful evidence that people who identify strongly with a particular set of cultural experiences often do choose to consult counsellors and psychotherapists who share these experiences'. The key aspect here is choice; young people may not have access to the resources that enable them to make such a choice.

In terms of what is available, many of the approaches for counselling young people assume a level of individual resourcefulness which may not be present. The experiences of marginalised young people will be varied and their capacity to effect change will be influenced by the social context within which they operate. Outside the cocoon of the counselling space, a young person's ability to make things happen in the larger context of their life will depend on their access to social and economic power.

REFLECTION POINT

- Many models used for counselling young people are premised on the humanist concept of the power of the individual to effect change in their lives. How well does that relate to the young people you work with or know? For whom may this approach be less effective?

A case study may be useful here to explore the point further.

Case study 4.1   Expecting to be told

Jaya is 16 years of age and has been referred by her tutor to her school counsellor as she seems increasingly anxious and her school work has been affected negatively. Her tutor has not been able to find out what is wrong. Gill, the counsellor, has seen Jaya three times and the issue is related to the pressure to achieve high grades in the forthcoming examinations. Gill is happy that trust and rapport are established and has remained person-centred throughout. She has taken time to explore the issue with Jaya, and at the last session they agreed one or two short-term goals and action. On her fourth visit Gill asks Jaya how she got on with the agreed action and is disappointed when she learns that Jaya has not taken any of the agreed steps.

Gill: 'What stopped you Jaya?'
Jaya: 'I dunno really.'
Gill: 'Well, we agreed that the action steps would be useful – perhaps I got that wrong?"
Jaya (shrugs): 'Yeah, we did, but . . .I dunno . . .'
Gill: 'Go on Jaya, tell me what you're thinking, so that I understand.'
Jaya: 'Well, I thought you were the expert not me – I agreed to come here because I thought you could help and tell me what was the best thing to do.'
Gill: 'Ah, I see – I should have made that more clear. I wanted you to decide based on what you think is important for you, rather than what I think is important.'
Jaya: 'But it is my family who will decide what is important, once we know what the best thing is to do.'

ACTIVITY 4.2

- Having read the case study, think about the assumptions that Gill made in the previous sessions and what she can do now to take forward the work with Jaya.
- When you have finished reading the chapter, review your thoughts about what action might be useful for both Jaya and Gill.

THE MULTICULTURAL APPROACH WITHIN COUNSELLING AND PSYCHOTHERAPY

The importance of understanding the client's cultural and social context is emphasised in multicultural counselling (Sue et al., 1996) and (like this book) supports an integrated approach. An integrated approach moves away from the idea that there is one way of doing things and advocates the use of particular strategies as relevant to the client's needs.

This leads to a collaborative relationship where negotiated decisions are made about what works best for the client. A multicultural approach will help practitioners to understand their clients' real rather than presumed needs.

(Reid, 2005, p175)

Collaboration is a key word – and it is worth commenting on language here as the language of 'helping' itself puts the young person in the subservient position in terms of the power of the helper. Working alongside a young person, asking 'how can I be useful?' rather than 'how can I help?' is a good place to start in the establishment of an approach that is anti-oppressive.

Clearly, the counsellor's view of what is useful may not coincide with that of a young person whose life experience is very different; even when they may both be part of the same cultural group. Values are formed by socialisation in the family (whatever form that takes) and the community, and a view of what might be possible in the present and future will be constructed by the individual according to their own perceptions of what is possible. With support, the original counselling goal may alter as the interest and circumstances begin to change, in the way that horizons shift and open up for people on the move. It is important to be mindful that goals differ and are culturally based.

Arulmani (2009) suggests there is a need to develop a 'cultural preparedness' approach to counselling interventions, attuned to the ways of thinking and being within a particular cultural context. In terms of youth counselling in the West, the aspirations of young people from 'minority communities' are likely to reflect strongly held beliefs that are different from the dominant culture. This point is worth bearing in mind for both newly arrived and second- and third-generation young people from a number of minority groups. However, the issue is complex. Young people from minority communities may rebel against the beliefs and values of their community and want to adopt the cultural beliefs of the dominant culture. Assuming a set of cultural beliefs based on membership of a particular group is itself a kind of tyranny. Further, these observations are not restricted to issues relating to ethnicity. They also highlight that when aiming for social justice, solutions taken to fit the 'problems' of one group, because they are seen to be 'what works', may not be transferable to another.

REFLECTION POINT

- In what ways are your cultural beliefs and practices different from your parents' or those of your community? Why?

DEFINING EQUAL OPPORTUNITY AND SOCIAL JUSTICE

As the above discussion indicates, working towards practice that is anti-oppressive is complex and we need to think about the terms we use. The concept of equal opportunity, for instance, suggests that the same access to opportunity is sufficient to create equality. The concept of social justice moves beyond a simplistic approach to equality and promotes a vision of society where the distribution of social benefits is based on fairness. This rejects the notion of 'the same for all' and recognises that the disadvantaged within any society will need more than, not the same as, others. An unthinking 'same for all' approach can lead to the recommendation of practices based on assumptions about shared goals and values. In other words, a view that there is one universally held goal, rather than a number of diverse goals of equal value. This view seeks to adapt 'different' behaviour to fit with the prevailing discourse (accepted ways of talking and thinking about a subject) in any society about what is 'normal'.

When counselling young people we need to be clear about what we are trying to do with the young person in terms of the wider context in which we, as the counsellor, operate. There can be an external pressure (from an agency, often related to how that agency is funded) to measure progress against educational or vocational outcomes, not just behavioural goals. Such measurements are often used to justify a service, but may not be relevant to the young person's counselling needs at that time. Keeping the young person's goals in the forefront is paramount, but such demands can place a strain on our desire to remain person-centred. This is not to say that any goal is acceptable when there are behaviours and actions which are viewed as unacceptable within the moral codes and justice systems in most contexts, for example a violent attack on another person. That said, situational 'definitions' will differ (self defence?), but space precludes a further discussion here.

Consequently, although focused on difference, if there is an assumption in policies of equal opportunities that difference does not challenge a dominant Western ideology, then the experiences of many marginalised young people can become depoliticised, devalued and hidden. By contrast, a critical approach would work to expose the hidden processes that ensure that marginalised groups remain on the periphery despite the good intentions of policies to promote equality of opportunity (Kincheloe and Steinberg, 1997). Thinking that youth counselling can be a neutral activity detached from 'politics' is flawed. Exclusion is endemic in all modern (and postmodern) societies and the limitations of inclusion based on notions of equal opportunities via increasing individual 'employability', the redistribution of wealth or cultural assimilation and integration, need to be examined (Levitas, 2005). Counselling of the individual young person does not operate outside of the wider social context.

The preceding discussion is important, but if navigating the perilous waters of multiculturalism is presented as too difficult, what is to be done? The counsellor working with diverse individuals cannot possibly understand the experiences of all young people who inhabit a range of cultural groups. And is this desirable in any case? A detailed study of a particular ethnic group or an examination of the life experiences of a young person who is gay or disabled will be insightful, but is, once again, consigning individuals to one-dimensional categories into which they are unlikely to fit.

Instead of searching for solutions to the implied problem of how to 'deal with' a young person who is a member of a socially disadvantaged group, the work needs to be approached from a different perspective.

Counselling agencies working with a range of young people are, of course, sensitive to the need for multicultural awareness. Yet, multicultural aware-ness without an exploration of the contested ideas about race and culture can be an afterthought and may be viewed by the counsellor as something else to learn about – another training module or course to find time for. If we understand multiculturalism to be wider than ethnicity, where are the boundaries drawn around what the counsellor needs to know? As indicated above, an approach that assigns people to categories such as BME (Black and Minority Ethnic), Muslim, gay, school truant, substance user, additional needs, abused, homeless or NEET (not in education, employment or train-ing) and so on – fixes young people in assumed one-dimensional char-acterisations which are useful for agencies and those that fund agency work, but cannot encompass the person to whom the label is applied. This is not their whole story, but it is how they become defined by others who have the power to categorise them in this way and the label then may become self-fulfilling.

> *The deterministic and essentialist quality of these assumptions has the potential to evoke feelings of helplessness and reduce people's abilities to act.*
>
> (Monk et al., 2008, xv)

Case study 4.2   Focusing on the problem rather than the person

Joseph is an experienced counsellor who has worked with young men with drug addictions for a number of years. Andy sees him for the first time in an outreach youth centre to talk about the impact his drug taking is having on his relationships. Having heard Andy's story about the drug taking, Joseph uses his knowledge and extensive networks to plan a programme for behavioural change that will help to reduce Andy's use of drugs, with the aim of being addiction free in the future.

Joseph is pleased that Andy is keen to engage in the counselling programme, which includes group sessions with other young people with the same problem. Andy leaves, picking up his guitar and a box of CDs that he left with the receptionist. 'Is that you, Andy, on the front of those CDs?' she asks.

REFLECTION POINT

- What is your immediate reaction to the case study above?

The philosophical perspective that underpins the approach to multiculturalism can be summarised by White's (1989, p7) statement, introduced at the beginning of the chapter: 'The person is not the problem; the problem is the problem.'

In terms of youth counselling, the young person should not be defined as problematic as this merely creates an 'us and them' approach which ignores the reasons underlying the issue. It is important that the young person's needs are identified, but at the point of intervention the core condition of respect for their view of the world should lead the counsellor to question the assumptions they have made about the perceived 'group' membership. We need to be wary of statements (and actions) that create further division whether made by those who offer support; for example, 'We all want the same things, someone who cares about us, a job and security, and this is the way I can help you', or those who are on the receiving end of such 'help', for example, 'You can't help, as you don't know what it's like to be me'.

REFLECTION POINT

- In your working context how is the 'problem behaviour of young people' defined? Why is it defined in that way – who defines it?

Having made the point that goals differ and should not be assumed by any perceived group membership, it should be clear by now that it is not the intention to suggest a cookbook of recipes for working with specific individuals. What the chapter will now do is work towards a usable definition of social constructionism as the bedrock for a multicultural approach, and then it will consider multicultural principles that can be embedded for counselling young people. The purpose is to provide practical suggestions of how such an approach can lead to practice that is anti-oppressive. In other words, a promotion of 'good' practice that challenges social discrimination and oppression (Thompson, 1993) beyond a rather sterile list of multicultural competency standards that must be met.

SOCIAL CONSTRUCTIONISM AND THE SIGNIFICANCE OF MEANING

When trying to define terms such as social constructionism, we can get lost in an academic 'hall of mirrors' that includes other postmodern and post-structuralist concepts that make problematic everyday terms and assumptions. It is important to question assumptions and strategies which are viewed as 'common sense', but we do need to get on! Thus, the definition that follows is partial and reductive, but will set the scene for what comes next.

Postmodern refers to a 'post-industrial' age where explanations of the world and our place within it cannot be accounted for by scientific reasoning alone. Poststructuralist explanations attempt to show, through a detailed historical analysis, how social systems have come to operate in the way they do. Social systems include health and education provision, social welfare, policing, and so on – within which we are all socialised and 'disciplined'. Within such systems individuals – subjects – are formed within discourses that establish what social roles are possible and impossible. Discourses, in terms of how to speak and who can speak, and what can be said, are constrained by discursive boundaries based on what counts as truth, knowledge, cultural values and socially defined norms of behaviour (Britzman, 2000).

Definitions for social constructionism vary, but Monk et al. offer the following based on Gergen's contributions within psychology (1994):

> *Social constructionism (some argue that the word social is redundant) points to the way our experiences are constructed rather than determined in advance as part of the natural working out of biological processes.*
>
> (2008, p5)

People develop their understandings of the social world in relationships with others. The meanings they take from those experiences shape their values, identity and the way they act within the world, and are evident in the way they speak about themselves and others. The discourses that influence an individual's view of self and others can be heard in the underlying assumptions about concepts that are often taken to have shared meaning, when in many cases, these are culturally bound.

A good opportunity, says who?

In the context of discussing education, training and work, what does the word 'opportunity' mean?

Vocational counsellor Sam: 'This is a three-week short course that gives you an opportunity to develop skills that you could transfer to a full-time job. You would get the training allowance and then you could write it on your CV.'

'NEET' young person Chaz: thinks – you're having a laugh, I can earn more than that in a couple of hours helping Nick sell his stuff!

Reflecting on the above example, the policy maker, service manager and the counsellor may have different views on how achievable it is for many young people to be economically active and independent. Their views are informed by different and often competing discourses. But for a young person, living in a location where there is endemic unemployment or underemployment, the promise of an allowance to enter further education or training may not be viewed as a viable 'opportunity' when much more can be gained within the illegal or informal economy. So, working with young people to develop counselling goals must take account of what is personally meaningful for them. Failure to integrate goals and opportunities with what young people view as relevant will not motivate them to any sustainable action. This is not to ignore the wider social context and social norms within which a young person must operate: esteem for others needs as much attention as the development of self-esteem. What is suggested here is a need to examine how the young person constructs their view of the world. This also means that the counsellor will need to question their own 'taken for granted' views about the world and the purposes, processes and outcomes of youth counselling.

Thus, whether in the role of counsellor or client, what you see depends on where you stand to look: to see differently you need to be prepared to shift your position. The multiculturally aware practitioner will be cognisant of their own prejudices with regard to any aspect of social disadvantage. While this may be a useful starting point, it does not allow for an investigation into *why* those prejudices exist. In the same way as suggesting that without a consideration of the wider social context an individualistic approach to problem solving will remove inequalities for a young person – 'take this course, change your attitude, find a job, find a new group of friends' – instructing a counsellor to be 'more self-aware' is also limited. A deeper analysis is required.

Culture is a social construction, created through language and used to classify people – it is not a fixed truth and it changes over time. For example, consider how cultural views towards homosexuality have changed over the last thirty years in the 'mainstream' culture of the UK. When working with a young person in a counselling context we need to think about how many times they have been defined by others. They arrive with stories told about them and, previous to entering a counselling relationship, are rarely given the time and opportunity to present their own view of themselves to an authentic listener. A counsellor who recognises the roots of their own world view and understands the reasons for these without blaming self or others, is in a better position to open up and respond to a young person who does not fit into rigid preconceived categories. To show respectful curiosity in a genuine wish to understand the story the young person would like to tell about themselves, is more likely to build and maintain rapport and trust, and achieve an effective and collaborative working relationship.

REFLECTION POINT

- Recall an example where the cultural messages from your background were in conflict with those demonstrated by a young person with whom you were working. What happened? Why?

COMMENT

What the discussion above suggests is that the counsellor needs knowledge of more than one model of intervention. As noted in the opening chapter in this book, the selective mining of counselling approaches that have varying philosophical and theoretical backgrounds is seen by many as questionable. An eclectic approach can lead to a partial understanding where both the counsellor and young person can get lost when only a surface knowledge of the model becomes apparent (Reid, 2008). However, as argued in Chapter 2, an integrative approach explores a range of theories and models, beyond a superficial understanding. The aim is to meet the diverse needs of young people, in order to understand the young person's perspective and the meanings they construct about themselves and their place in the world. In other words, adopting a singular approach may not result in effective interventions for what are complex 'life' decisions. So, when working with a range of young people from diverse 'communities' (in the widest sense), what are the principles that need to be embedded into practice?

MULTICULTURAL PRINCIPLES FOR PRACTICE

Sue et al. (1995) have developed a detailed matrix for what they view as cross-cultural skills for those working in counselling. Their classification focuses on aspects of beliefs and attitudes, knowledge and skills, and is organised under three headings.

1   Awareness of own assumptions, values and beliefs.
2   Understanding the worldview of the 'culturally different' client.
3   Developing appropriate intervention techniques and strategies.

The reflexive questions that are posed in this chapter should help with the examination of beliefs and attitudes, and aid the development of knowledge and skills. Further activities that can be useful include: reading; visits to extend knowledge of diverse groups; collaborating with clients to hear their stories; small-scale qualitative research with clients on particular issues; presentations to share experiences with colleagues; discussions in supervision; reflective and reflexive journal writing; observations of the use of different models, methods and techniques; finding creative ways of hearing and understanding the 'voices' of diverse young people, for example through art, craft, music, theatre and poetry.

Mindful that meaning is culturally based, if we take 'principles' to mean principled action informed by praiseworthy behaviour based on a moral code (in other words, a concept that is stronger than 'guidelines' to be followed, or not), then principles that are informed by the matrix offered by Sue et al. could include the following:

- awareness of own biases and limitations and their outcomes;
- recognition of the range of social variables that lead to cultural difference;
- knowledge about the causes and effects of oppression, racism, discrimination and stereotyping;
- openness about the processes of counselling young people with a view to a collaborative approach that works alongside the young person;
- commitment to enriching understanding through continuous professional and reflexive development;
- searching for appropriate and culturally sensitive models of intervention, rather than reliance on established or 'singular' methods;
- awareness and understanding of the impact of negative treatment experienced by marginalised groups;
- commitment to outreach work;
- respect for young people's beliefs, values and views about themselves and the stories they choose to tell the counsellor;
- value for the language, style and manner of speech, while acknowledging there will be times when the counsellor's linguistic skills will be inadequate;
- questioning of the appropriateness and helpfulness of organisational assessment methods;
- awareness of institutional practices that lead to discrimination;
- congruence when advocating with, or lobbying on behalf of, young people to overcome relevant discrimination;

- understanding of the differences in communication styles and their impact, plus extension of own communication skills and methods;
- open-mindedness to alternative ways of supporting, including using the resources of the young person's community.

ACTIVITY 4.3

- Which of the above principles do you need to work on? Why and how? What activities will you undertake? Make some notes. If useful, you could turn these into an action plan.

It is also important to add to the list the avoidance of essentialist thinking:

> *Essentialism is the habit of thought that invites people to always look for explanations in the intrinsic essence of things or of persons rather than the cultural influences like narratives.*
>
> (Winslade and Monk, 2008, p6)

In other words, attributing certain behaviour as 'natural' when ascribing individuals to groups. An example would be that young people who are NEET (not in education, employment or training) are 'not motivated', 'cannot get up in the morning' and so on because they are 'NEET'. This is more than stereotyping as it assumes that a person's feelings or beliefs are *essential to who they are*, whereas 'who they are' will depend on a range of factors aside from being categorised as NEET. The label is a construction, not a natural essence, and while it may have real effects on the young person's behaviour and on the behaviour of others towards them, it is not a fixed state and is subject to change. Essentialist thinking suggests that we can be described in singular terms that fit snugly into cultural categories. These ideas are returned to in a later chapter.

CHAPTER SUMMARY

This chapter has engaged in definitions and offered multicultural principles for practice. To extend the aim of embedding multicultural thinking, a number of questions were posed. These reflexive questions were designed to assist the reader to locate their own position with regard to some of the issues raised and to consider previous assumptions they may not have examined before. Before concluding the chapter a final set of reflexive questions is posed – once again, note down your responses.

ACTIVITY 4.4

- The subject of multiculturalism can raise sensitive issues – what sensitivities were evident for you when reading this chapter? Has your thinking shifted at all – if so, in what way?
- How would you promote multicultural principles and anti-oppressive practice in your counselling practice? Think beyond the policies and lists of competencies that may be in place – specifically, what else would you like to do?

This chapter has referred earlier to the principle of open-mindedness. It is a term that is familiar and could sum up the aim of the chapter. Bruner uses the term and its simplicity has an elegance that relates well to the ethos of multicultural counselling practice.

> *I take open-mindedness to be a willingness to construe knowledge and values from multiple perspectives without loss of commitment to one's own values. Open-mindedness is the keystone of what we call a democratic culture. We have learned, with much pain, that democratic culture is neither divinely ordained nor is it to be taken for granted as perennially durable. Like all cultures, it is premised upon values that generate distinctive ways of life and corresponding conceptions of reality . . . I take the constructivism of cultural psychology to be a profound expression of democratic culture. It demands that we be conscious of how we come to our knowledge and as conscious as we can be about the values that lead us to our perspectives.*
>
> (Bruner, 1990, p30)

SUGGESTED FURTHER READING

Bruner, J (1990) *Acts of Meaning*. Cambridge, Massachusetts: Harvard University Press.

Bruner is not writing specifically on multicultural counselling, but this is a seminal, beautifully written, understandable and short text that provides insight into philosophical and ethical concepts that are important for a multicultural approach.

Monk, G, Winslade, J and Sinclair, S (2008) *New Horizons in Multicultural Counselling*. Thousand Oaks, California: Sage Publications.

This book is both accessible and comprehensive. The authors have an engaging style and, like this book, use reflective exercises throughout the work.

Parker, I (2007) *Revolution in Psychology: Alienation to Emancipation.* London: Pluto Press.

This book takes a critical approach to psychology, highlighting the assumptions embedded in many approaches. It provides the cautionary insight that all reflexive practitioners need. It is at times a challenging read, but worth the effort.

CHAPTER 5

Using transactional analysis to develop effective communication in counselling young people

by Jane Westergaard

CORE KNOWLEDGE

By the end of this chapter you will have the opportunity to:

- identify the key principles underpinning transactional analysis;
- understand the impact of communication on the lives of young people;
- reflect on effective communication in your own counselling practice.

INTRODUCTION

While person-centred, cognitive-behavioural, solution-focused, narrative approaches and other orientations introduced in this book offer the counsellor a particular philosophical and psychological approach to their counselling practice, transactional analysis (TA) developed by Berne (1964) suggests something slightly different. Where the approaches mentioned above promote a 'way of being' with young people, and offer strategies and techniques to effect change, TA provides a way in which transactions (communications) between counsellor and client can be analysed. This analysis informs the counsellor's understanding of the young person and helps to develop effective communication between them. In addition, and perhaps more importantly when counselling young people, TA can be used to offer insight and invite reflection on the part of the client with regard to how they communicate with others, and the consequences that this might have in their lives.

Berne's background was in psychoanalysis. He practised initially from a Freudian, psychodynamic perspective, but began to distance himself from Freud's work and develop his own ideas, which, he hoped were more accessible than pure psychodynamic thinking. McLeod explains:

> The central innovation in TA has been the replacement of the Freudian superego-id-ego structure with a model consisting of three 'ego states':

parent, adult and child. The use of everyday language here, as in other parts of TA theory, serves to demystify psychodynamic ideas and make them more accessible and relevant to ordinary people.

(2003, p192)

So, this chapter begins by setting out the key principles of transactional analysis and considers, in particular, the concept of the three ego states mentioned above in the light of understanding and counselling young people. The chapter will go on to focus in a practical way on how TA can be used effectively to inform counselling practice.

It should be noted at this early point that there are a number of key elements to TA in addition to ego states. Berne emphasised the importance of a range of concepts including *scripts* – creating a life-script for ourselves at a young age which we continue to play out through our lives; *game playing* – using communication to get what we want or need, but not necessarily in an open and assertive way; *rackets* – substituting one feeling for another, for example sadness and anger are often mistaken for each other; *strokes* – seeking recognition or attention in order to receive a positive or negative 'stroke' from another. Rather than attempt to cover these important concepts superficially, additional reading is suggested at the end of the chapter which will provide further insight.

This chapter will focus specifically on the concept of ego states and life positions, in order to gain greater understanding about the ways in which young people communicate both with the counsellor and with others in their lives. This in turn informs the development of more assertive and appropriate transactions.

THE PRINCIPLES OF TRANSACTIONAL ANALYSIS

As has already been suggested, Eric Berne set out to make more accessible (but not necessarily to simplify) some complex psychodynamic concepts. The term 'transactional analysis' refers to the ways in which individuals 'transact' or communicate with each other. TA attempts to analyse, or understand, how each individual adheres to particular patterns of communication, learned and developed in childhood, in order to have their needs met. Observation of clients with whom he worked suggested to Berne that a transaction (communication) takes place in two ways: we use words which are selected consciously to convey thoughts and feelings (social level) and we communicate on a deeper (often unconscious) level through tone of voice, facial expression and demeanour (psychological level). Sometimes, though, the social and psychological are in conflict and communication is incongruent. It is the tension between *what* is being said and *how* it is being said that provides rich material for counsellors and clients to work with.

Berne identified the psychological level of communication as coming from one of three discrete 'ego states'. He described these ego states as Parent, Adult and Child. More on this later.

REFLECTION POINT

- Think of a time when the words you said were actually in conflict with what you meant. How did you communicate what you were *really* feeling at the psychological level?

The case study below shows Meena, the teenage pregnancy counsellor introduced in Chapter 3, working with a client, **Susie**, whose verbal and non-verbal messages (social and psychological communication) are in conflict.

Case study 5.1   Social and psychological communication in conflict

Meena: 'So, Susie, how are you feeling today?'

Susie (slumped in chair, looking down at the floor and twisting the strap of her handbag round and round in her hands): 'OK . . . Fine.'

Meena (using the skill of immediacy): 'You say you're feeling fine, but it looks to me as though that's not the whole story.'

Susie (defensively): 'Yeah, well I *am* fine, so I don't know why you're saying that.' (Susie looks away).

Meena: 'I guess it's because you seem quite down. You're saying you're fine but everything about the way you're sitting here with me suggests that you're not feeling fine at all. In fact, to me, you look really fed up.'

Susie (shrugging her shoulders): 'Well I don't know where you get that idea from. I might just be a bit tired, that's all. I don't want to talk about it.' (Again, Susie looks away.)

Meena: 'OK, Susie. It's fine if you don't want to talk about how you're feeling today, but maybe it would help you if you could talk about what's going on for you. How would you like to use this session?'

COMMENT

In the case study above, Susie is demonstrating to Meena exactly how she is feeling, but this is not what she is expressing verbally. Her non-verbal communication is in direct conflict with the words she is using. The tension between the social and psychological levels of communication is providing the counsellor with a strong message.

REFLECTION POINT

• What might you pick up from Susie's demeanour? Is Meena right to challenge this inconsistency with Susie?

TA suggests that it is important to examine and reflect on our psychological as well as our social communication, to ensure that we are able to meet our needs in an honest and open way. This is not always easy (as the example above demonstrates), but choosing to ignore the psychological communication would not be a helpful response.

It has been proposed (see McLeod above) that Berne's ego states (Parent, Adult and Child) relate to Freud's superego, id and ego. The concept of the superego, id and ego lies at the heart of Freud's hypothesis about the significance of the unconscious and the power that the unconscious exerts in all areas of our lives, informing our thoughts, feelings and actions. The view that Berne's ego states derive directly from Freud's three concepts is not universally shared, however. Stewart and Joines state:

> The resemblance between the two models is not surprising, given that Berne was trained initially as a Freudian analyst . . . [but] . . . in his early writings Berne was at pains to point out the differences between his model and that of Freud's.
>
> (1987, p17)

As Berne made clear, there are significant differences in approach, but what remains consistent is the acceptance of the role played by the unconscious. And it is our psychological response through Berne's three ego states – Parent, Adult, Child – that is of interest here. Before examining each of these ego states in more detail and considering how communication from each might 'play out' in practice, it is helpful to establish the key philosophical features underpinning TA. Steiner (1990), Lister-Ford (2002), Clarkson (2005), Cornell and Hargaden (2005) and Widdowson (2009), each describe in detail the principles at the heart of TA. They are as follows:

• individuals have worth, value, rights and dignity;
• individuals have the capacity and capability for thought;
• individuals make decisions about their destiny and these decisions can be changed.

Like the person-centred approach (see Chapter 3) TA is rooted in a positive standpoint where the strength, rights and worth of individuals are valued. The approach is intrinsically optimistic about human nature, suggesting that resources for change are present in all of us, while recognising that we may make decisions which can be unproductive or even damaging. But remember, Berne would suggest that every decision can be changed and thus individuals can change too. Counsellors share this view, and this belief is often what keeps us committed to the work.

REFLECTION POINT

- What is your initial response to TA?
- What questions do you have in your mind when you consider the principles of the approach outlined above?
- To what extent do these principles underpin your own counselling practice?

THE EGO STATES

So far in this chapter a number of references have been made to Berne's ego states. As it is the concept of ego states that is central to TA, it is worth taking some time to establish what, exactly, Berne meant when he developed the idea of the Parent, Adult and Child ego states. (Notice in the discussion below how the ego states are written with a capital letter. This distinguishes them as a 'conceptual' rather than an 'actual' parent, adult or child.)

Put simply, Berne suggested that we have access to three ego states from which we communicate. Stewart and Joines explain that an ego state is 'a set of related behaviors, thoughts and feelings. It is a way in which we manifest a part of our personality at a given time' (1996, p4). It is important to note that there is a time dimension associated with each ego state. An individual communicating in the Parent ego state is 'acting out' responses that have been learned by observing a parent or parental figure's behaviour in the *past*. Communication in the Child ego state is when an individual replays responses from their own *past* in order to have their needs met. By contrast, an individual in the Adult ego state is responding directly and assertively to the 'here and now', thereby acting in the *present*. Therefore, two of the three ego states are firmly located in the past experiences of the individual. Only the Adult ego state resides in the present. It is also crucial to remember that the ego states are intensely personal. Our individual observations of parents and what we learn from them will differ from person to person. That said, there are certain 'common' features which characterise communication from the Parent ego state. So what are the features of each ego state and from where do they derive?

Parent ego state

As stated above, the Parent ego state is learned, from birth, and is a manifestation of our observations of our own parent's or parental figure's, behaviour and responses. This ego state is subdivided into two: the *Critical Parent* (CP) and the *Nurturing Parent* (NP). Communication from the Critical Parent ego state is likely to be characterised by a sharp tone of voice, a pointing finger, a stern expression. For example, 'don't you *ever* do that again!' or 'you're late again! You must make sure you're here on time in future.' Every child will recognise when their parent is angry or trying to control their behaviour in some way. Every adult will recognise this Critical Parent communication in others too. As with all the ego states, it is important to identify the times when we may communicate from our Critical Parent in order to get what we want – and the effect that this may have on others. It is worth noting that often communication from Critical Parent is at the expense of the person we are communicating with (as seen in the examples above). Communicating from our Critical Parent might get us what we want in the short term, but may leave the person we are communicating with feeling hurt, upset or even damaged in some way.

The Nurturing Parent is very different in tone from the Critical Parent, but is learned in exactly the same way through observation of parents and parental figures as a child. A response coming from a Nurturing Parent ego state might sound like this, 'oh, you poor thing, come here and I'll sort it out for you,' or 'tell me all about it and I'll make sure that never happens again.' The Nurturing Parent ego state is often characterised by gentleness of tone, softness of facial expression and openness of body posture. Communication from the Nurturing Parent suggests a 'there, there, let me make it better' response which can appear comforting, but is not necessarily helpful in enabling the recipient to manage their life more effectively for themselves. Steiner (1990) summarises the Parent ego state neatly, describing it as tape recorder which contains a selection of messages from a parent or significant authority figure (some helpful, others not) that we can replay at any time.

ACTIVITY 5.1

- Reflect on the last week and write down the times in your day-to-day relationships when you communicated from your own Critical Parent or Nurturing Parent ego state. What did this communication look/sound like? What does this tell you about the circumstances when you may find yourself communicating psychologically from the Parent ego state? With whom?
- Now, what might be the implications of communicating from either Critical or Nurturing Parent in the counselling room with young people?

COMMENT

It goes without saying that the way we communicate in counselling is likely to have an impact on our clients. Responding to a client from a Critical Parent ego state may contribute to feelings of defensiveness or fear in the young person (it may also be exactly the response they are expecting – or even wanting – from an adult). Alternatively, a Nurturing Parent response may feel warm, safe and comforting to a young person, but may not be a particularly helpful response. Ultimately, communication from both Critical and Nurturing Parent in counselling may serve to disempower rather than empower young clients.

Child ego state

As with the Parent, transactions from the Child ego state present from two different perspectives: the Free Child (FC) and the Adapted Child (AC). Communication from our Free Child (FC) is spontaneous, curious, creative or rebellious. A typically Free Child response might sound like this: 'OK, the sun's shining. Let's forget about going to work today and go to the beach instead!' or 'There's no way anyone is going to tell me what to do, it's my life, it's up to me!' By contrast, in the Adapted Child (AC) ego state, communications stem from a willingness to please, to agree and to 'do the right thing'. Someone responding to the two Free Child examples above from their Adapted Child might say to the first, 'I'd love to go to the beach, but I don't want to get into trouble and get told off,' and to the second, 'I wish I could do what I want like you, but I'm afraid that life's just not like that for me.' It is important to remind ourselves that we have access to our Child ego state as adults. Of course, this can (and should) be positive. For example, when a young child asks us to play a game with them, our Child ego state enables us to abandon ourselves and join in wholeheartedly. Or when our friends suggest a spur-of-the-moment night out, we should be able to say 'go for it!' But there are times when we find our Child voice rebelling or seeking approval and this can be disempowering and unhelpful.

REFLECTION POINT

- When might we respond in our Child ego state? Can you think of a time recently when you communicated from your Child ego state? What prompted the communication from Child rather than Adult? Who were you communicating with? Does this often happen with this person?
- Can you think of clients who frequently respond in their Child? What effect does this have on you as the counsellor?

When one person transacts with another from a particular ego state (in this case, Child), it is likely to have a direct impact on how the listener responds. Someone communicating from their Child is likely to elicit either a Parent or a Child response. It is important for counsellors to be aware of the power of what Berne called *complementary transactions*. We will explore the possible impact of this in counselling in more detail later.

Adult ego state

The third ego state is that of Adult. Transactions from the Adult ego state suggest a logical, rational and assertive response, firmly rooted in the 'here and now'. When communication stems from our Adult it will be reasoned, clear and underpinned by a sense of self-responsibility. We have access to all three ego states from around the age of 10 to 12 years. This means that most young people are capable of communicating from their Adult. Colledge explains that the 'Adult or neopsychic ego state autonomously and objectively appraises reality and makes judgements' (2002, p102). So, a counsellor's response from an Adult ego state to a client in their Child, might sound like this: 'I'm conscious of what a difficult time you are going through right now. How might we work together on this?'

Harris helps us to understand the concept of all three ego states further:

> *When the Parent or Child dominates, the outcome is predictable . . . When the Adult is in charge of the transaction, the outcome is not always predictable. There is the possibility of failure, but there is also the possibility of success. Most importantly, there is the possibility of change.*
> (1995, p58)

There is helpful guidance in this quote for those who are involved in counselling relationships with young people. Often, counsellors are transacting with young people who are presenting from their Parent or Child ego state. These young people are frequently communicating from an emotional rather than a rational position, either seeking approval or resisting it (Child) or playing back messages received earlier in life (Parent). The implication of Harris's words are that counsellors, where possible, should try to remain in their Adult ego state to enable change to occur. This kind of transaction (for example, Child to Adult, or Adult to Parent) is not complementary and is described by Berne as a 'crossed' transaction. Examples of crossed transactions are given later in this chapter.

REFLECTION POINT

- Think of a client with whom you have worked recently who communicated, for the most part, in their Child or Parent ego state. What are the signs that suggest to you they were communicating in Child or Parent? How did you 'transact' with them (from which ego state)? Was this a complementary transaction (Parent to Child, Child to Parent, Parent to Parent or Child to Child)? If yes, what impact might transacting in the Adult ego state have had?

It is important to recognise and embrace the value of all three ego states. By emphasising the benefits of communicating from the Adult ego state in counselling, it is not the intention to suggest that we should aspire to communicate from our Adult ego state at all times. How boring life would be if this was the case. There may be times when a Nurturing or Critical Parent response is appropriate in our lives. Similarly, we would not want to lose touch with our inner Child. But it is helpful to understand the impact that communication from our own ego state (whatever that might be) may have on clients.

To summarise, Stewart (2000) explains how knowledge of the ego state model is useful. In brief he suggests the following.

- Identification of the ego state from which a client is transacting can be made reliably through questioning and observation.
- Counsellors are able to judge on an on-going basis whether clients are replaying their childhood (Child), accessing communication learned from parent or parental figures (Parent) or responding directly in the here and now (Adult).
- Counsellors who understand and can identify their own ego states, are able to monitor their responses to clients.
- Counsellors with this knowledge can help themselves and their clients to *choose* which response they want to make (they are therefore in control of their communication).

TRANSACTIONAL ANALYSIS IN COUNSELLING PRACTICE

Having been introduced to the concept of TA in general and the ego states in particular, how might TA inform the work of counsellors working with young people? It is important for counsellors to recognise not only *what* young clients are saying to them, but also the *way* in which they are communicating. The tone of voice, and visual and non-verbal clues will offer insight into the meaning behind the words (the psychological level of communication with which counsellors should engage). The counsellor will recognise the young person's ego state by being alert to their own feelings and responses. The examples below show three complementary transactions in counselling. How effective might these transactions be?

In the first example, a young person communicates in their Adapted Child (AC) which has encouraged a complementary Nurturing Parent (NP) response from the counsellor:

Young Person: 'I'm really trying my best here, but it feels as though everyone is against me' (AC)
Counsellor: 'I know. Poor old you. Don't worry. Let me try and sort this out for you. (NP)

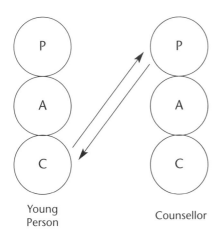

Figure 5.1
Young Person = Adapted Child and
Counsellor = Nurturing Parent

Likewise, in the second example, an inexperienced counsellor who is feeling unsettled, anxious and even fearful with a young person, may, on reflection, realise that they are working with a young person in their Critical Parent ego state.

Young Person: 'I've come to see you loads of times and still nothing gets sorted out. What's the point in counselling? It's a waste of time!' (CP)
Counsellor: 'Oh dear. I'm sorry about that. What else can I do to help?' (AC)

Alternatively, in the third example, the young person may be transacting in their Free Child, rebellious and uncontrolled, which may provoke a Critical Parent response from the counsellor:

Young Person: 'I don't care whether I get caught doing drugs or not. I'm having a great laugh with my mates.' (FC)
Counsellor: 'OK, but you can't go on like that forever, can you? (CP)

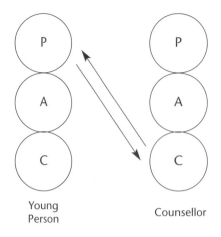

Figure 5.2
Young Person = Critical Parent and
Counsellor = Adapted Child

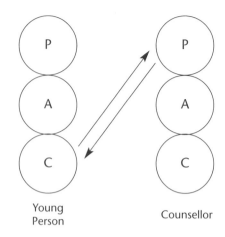

Figure 5.3
Young Person = Free Child and
Counsellor = Critical Parent

ACTIVITY 5.2

In each of the three examples above, what do you think might be the impact of the counsellor's response on the client and the ego state in which they are transacting?

• Read the section below and then identify and write down more helpful responses to each from the Adult ego state.

In each case in the examples above, it is likely that communication would continue to be 'stuck', where no change takes place and positions become increasingly entrenched. In counselling, the aim is to enable young people to reflect on their lives, consider options for change and make rational and informed decisions about those changes. This considered decision-making process is located firmly in the Adult ego state and it is therefore the role of the counsellor, among other things, to encourage young people to transact, when they can, from their Adult ego state.

An effective way to encourage communication from the Adult ego state is to 'cross' the transaction and communicate back in Adult to a young person transacting in their Child or Parent, rather than become 'hooked' into a 'complementary' response. As already explained, the examples outlined above show complementary transactions, Parent to Child and vice versa. By 'crossing' the transaction and responding to a Parent or Child in the Adult ego state, the natural pattern of the transaction will be broken and the young person should be encouraged to move from their Parent or Child to their Adult in order to restore a complementary Adult to Adult transaction. Once in their Adult ego state, functioning in the here and now, there is greater opportunity to consider situations rationally and reflect on the options for change systematically. The example below features **Janet**, an integrative counsellor working in a youth counselling agency. Janet remains in her Adult, while working with **Kirsty** who presents in her Child.

Case study 5.1   Crossing the transaction: Adult to Child

Janet: 'It sounds as though you are really angry with your mum today, Kirsty. Do you want to tell me what has happened?'

Kirsty: 'She's only gone and grounded me and taken away my mobile phone. It's not fair. I never even did anything wrong. I hate her.'

Janet: 'So you're angry because you think your mum is punishing you for something that you didn't do?'

Kirsty: 'It's not fair. She always picks on me. It's always my fault when things go wrong. She never has a go at my brother or sister. Always me. And now she's taken my phone. How does she think that's going to help?'

Janet: 'It seems like you're feeling really picked on right now. I wonder why you think that your mum is like this with you and not your brother or sister?'

Kirsty (angrily): 'I don't know, do I? Why don't you ask her?'

Janet (silence): 'I guess I'm asking you what *you* think, Kirsty.'

Kirsty (sighing): 'I don't know. It's just the way it is. It's always been the same. I'm the oldest, I get the blame. It's always my fault, never theirs. I can't do anything right as far as she's concerned.'

Janet: 'OK. Let's have a think about this. You're obviously very upset and, as I said just now, you're feeling unfairly treated and this makes you angry. Let's try to get to the bottom of what happened on this latest occasion that led to your mum grounding you and taking away your phone. Let's talk about what happened and try to understand what's going on here. How does that sound?'

Kirsty: 'What's the point? It won't make any difference, she'll still pick on me.'

Janet: 'OK, I hear what you're saying. But I've found that it can be helpful sometimes to talk about something that's happened and try to make sense of it. How about it? Shall we give it a try and see where we get to. What do you think?'

Kirsty: 'Alright. I suppose so . . .'

In the case study above, Janet works hard to remain in the Adult ego state. She ensures that Kirsty's anger has been heard and not dismissed, but she doesn't react in Parent or Child herself. This, over time, should provide Kirsty with the best opportunity for reflecting on her situation and her feelings about what has happened. This is a challenge for Janet and is not something that is easily or quickly achieved.

So, the aim then is to encourage communication between counsellor and young person in most cases, from the Adult ego state. As already stated, communication in Adult will be measured, thoughtful, rational and most effective in considering options, consequences and actions. If the counsellor can, in the main, transact from their Adult ego state and continue to do so throughout the interaction, this should encourage the young person, who may be communicating at a psychological level in Parent or Child, to move to their Adult.

It is important to note, that communicating in Adult does not suggest an unemotional and impersonal response to a client – quite the reverse. Warmth and empathy should be central to any interaction, but encouraging young people to engage from their Adult ego state will also ensure that the work is purposeful.

There is a danger when implementing any approach which appears to 'label' clients. The Parent, Adult and Child ego states are examples of labels which can be applied easily, but mistakenly. Care should be taken in analysing the non-verbal signals that are being received (and attention must be paid to cultural difference – see Chapter 4) in order to ensure that ego states are identified accurately.

In addition to providing a useful guide to communication between counsellor and young person, TA also offers the opportunity for young people to understand more about their own behaviour and communication, and the effect that this may have on others. Discussed sensitively, young people can grasp the significance of the consequences of transacting from an angry or defensive position (Parent or Child ego state), and they can be helped to find alternative ways to communicate their needs. Counsellors, too, should be alert to *their* preferred responses (Berne suggested that many of us have a 'dominant' ego state which is our 'default' position), constantly 'checking out' the ego state from which their own transactions are generated.

When working with young people there is always the risk that our Parent ego state is 'hooked'. It can be a challenge to avoid responding in Nurturing Parent to damaged and vulnerable young people who are presenting in Child. Indeed, it is a nurturing relationship that they desperately crave. Although the role of the counsellor is to build trusting, empathic relationships with young people, it should also be remembered that counselling aims to help young people to explore ways in which they are able to find appropriate sources for developing the nurturing relationships for which they are searching – and ultimately to nurture themselves.

ACTIVITY 5.3

Choose a client with whom you have worked over a number of sessions (again, it can be helpful to record a session – with your client's permission, of course).

- Can you identify the psychological level of communication? What is your client's dominant ego state? And how do you respond?
- Now that you have developed your understanding of TA, how might you work differently with this client? You may want to discuss your reflections in supervision.

COMMENT

The list below suggests some Adult ego state responses to the clients identified earlier in this chapter, thus 'crossing' the transaction.

- Client: 'I'm really trying my best here but it feels as though everyone is against me.'
- Counsellor: 'I'm sorry to hear that. I know how hard you're working at this. This is a very difficult time for you and I can see how unfair all of this must seem.'
- Client: 'I've come to see you loads of times and still nothing gets sorted out. What's the point in counselling? It's a waste of time!'
- Counsellor: 'I can hear how angry and frustrated you're feeling. It seems like you want me to wave a "magic wand" – and if I had one, I would! What would you like to happen – how might we go forward in these sessions?'
- Client: 'I don't care whether I get caught doing drugs or not. I'm having a laugh with my mates.'
- Counsellor: 'There's a bit of me that wants to say "you shouldn't be taking these risks", but I'm not sure how helpful that would be for you right now. Could we think about some of the implications of your lifestyle, short, medium and long term, and then you can decide whether or not you want to make any changes – even if they're small ones.'

ENCOURAGING YOUNG PEOPLE'S UNDERSTANDING

Earlier in the chapter, I suggested that TA is a useful concept not only for providing insight into communication in the counselling room, but also to assist young people to understand and reflect on how they communicate with others in their lives. A clearer understanding of the psychological messages they are relaying through their transactions in Parent, Adult or Child can help a young person to adapt and make choices about how they communicate. By so doing they should be able to get what they need more effectively and minimise the risk of provoking an unwanted response from the person with whom they are communicating. Harris (1995) suggests that Berne's concept of 'life positions' is important here. Harris identifies communication as stemming from one of four life positions. Table 5.1 sets out the four life positions and shows how they link to communication from the ego states.

I'm OK; You're OK	I'm OK; You're not OK
Assertive communication (I win, you win)	Aggressive communication (I win, you lose)
For example, Adult to Adult ego state	For example, Parent to Child ego state
I'm not OK; You're OK	I'm not OK; You're not OK
Passive communication (I lose, you win)	Manipulative communication (I lose, you lose)
For example, Child to Parent ego state	For example, Child to Parent ego state

Table 5.1 Life positions and ego states

Townend explains:

> *The challenge for everyone is to develop and maintain the healthy life position, I'm OK: You're OK, which is assertive/creative. In choosing this life position people are choosing to respect themselves and to develop relationships in which there is an underlying respect of other people and their differences.*
>
> (2007, p15)

What Townsend suggests is that an 'I'm OK; you're OK' life position is one to be aspired to and that communication from any of the other life positions may leave individuals (either the young person or those with whom they are communicating) feeling 'not OK'. Helping young people to reflect on the ways in which they communicate can be demanding and requires careful use of the skill of challenge. It can also be helpful to use the model identified above as a simple tool to engender greater understanding. The case study below returns to Janet and Kirsty.

Case study 5.2   Helping a young person to reflect on their own communication

Janet: 'Sometimes when we talk together, Kirsty, I get the feeling that you think I'm going to respond like you say your mum does and tell you off and blame you. Is that how you feel?'

Kirsty (silence): 'I don't understand. What do you mean?'

Janet: 'Well . . . for example, sometimes when you look at me, you seem quite angry. And when you speak you sound very defensive as though you're expecting me to tell you off and give you a hard time. Does this make sense to you?'

Kirsty: 'Kind of . . .'

Janet: 'I'm wondering if this is how you often respond to your mum or to other adults. You know, like you're expecting to be told off? And you're getting ready to defend yourself.'

Kirsty: 'Well, that's because they *do* tell me off. It's always my fault and I always get the blame. That's just how it is.'

Janet: 'Yes, you've often described how it feels. What I'm wondering is . . . is there a way that you might approach these people differently and show that you're not expecting to get into trouble. I don't mean that you should just agree with everything they say, but perhaps be more open to talking to them and putting your point over in a more positive way?'

Kirsty (doubtful): 'I could try, but I can't see how it would work.'

Janet: 'Well, how about if we have a go now? I could pretend to be someone – your mum or a teacher maybe? – and you try to respond to me in a positive, rather than aggressive way. Shall we give it a go and see how we get on?'

In the case study above, Janet is encouraging Kirsty to reflect on her pattern of psychological communication and to try to break the 'I'm not OK; you're OK' life position where she transacts largely from her Child.

REFLECTION POINT

- Can you identify clients with whom you work, who are entrenched in a particular life position, and interact from an 'I'm not OK; you're OK' perspective?
- What might you do in order to help your client to reflect on the implication of continuing to communicate in this way? How would you help them attempt to break the pattern that has formed?

CHAPTER SUMMARY

This chapter has introduced the concept of TA and examined in particular the suggestion that communication is on two levels – social and psychological. It has focused on the significance of the ego states in the following ways:

- how knowledge of ego states can influence more effective communication in the counselling room;
- how greater understanding of the ego states can assist young people to communicate from an 'I'm OK; you're OK' life position.

As explained at the start of this chapter, it has not been possible to examine every aspect of transactional analysis. However, the reading suggested below provides greater insight into an approach that informs, and can be integrated effectively into, counselling practice with young people.

SUGGESTED FURTHER READING

Harris, T (1995) *I'm OK – You're OK.* Reading: Arrow Books.

A seminal text, a little old-fashioned now, but still worthy of a glance.

Lister-Ford, C (2002) *Skills in Transactional Analysis Counselling and Psychotherapy.* London: Sage.

A practical book that examines the skills associated with a TA approach to counselling.

Newell, S and Jeffery, D (2002) *Behaviour Management in the Classroom: A Transactional Analysis Approach.* London: David Fulton.

Although this book is aimed at teachers rather than counsellors, it offers an insight into how TA can be used to understand communication between teachers and young people.

Sills, C and Hargarden, H (2002) *Ego States: Key Concepts in Transactional Analysis.* London: Worth Publishing.

A full, in-depth and detailed examination of the ego states which is a useful starting point for those interested in finding out more.

Stewart, I (2000) *Transactional Analysis in Action,* 2nd edition. London: Sage.

As with all the 'in Action' series, this book provides a sound and accessible introduction.

Widdowson, M (2009) *Transactional Analysis: 100 Key Points and Techniques.* London: Routledge.

Another good and practical guide, probably of more benefit to those who already have some counselling experience.

Transactional Analysis Journal, The International Transactional Analysis Association, California: USA (published quarterly).

This journal is a useful source of material reflecting up-to-date thinking and developments in TA.

CHAPTER 6

Understanding how cognitive behavioural approaches can inform counselling practice with young people

by Jane Westergaard

CORE KNOWLEDGE

By the end of this chapter you will have the opportunity to:

- identify the key principles underpinning cognitive behavioural therapy;
- reflect on the application of CBT to counselling practice;
- develop CBT strategies and techniques for your own counselling practice with young people.

INTRODUCTION

Cognitive behavioural therapy (CBT) is rapidly becoming one of the most popular forms of therapeutic intervention, particularly in the health sector (DH, 2008). Research (Roth and Fonagy, 1996; Kuyken, 2005; Ward et al., 2008) supports the view that therapy (and CBT in particular) can be a helpful and perhaps, as importantly, a cost-effective treatment for patients with a range of mental health and other medical problems. Colledge claims, 'a great advantage of cognitive therapy is that it is embedded in scientific method, so it is now being used to treat a growing range of disorders' (2002, p188).

In a book such as this which introduces the reader to a range of approaches to counselling, it would be remiss to exclude CBT. But it is not simply out of a sense of duty that CBT is included here. For counsellors working with young people who frequently experience distortions in their *cognitions* (thinking) and often exhibit unhelpful or limiting *behaviour*, CBT has much to offer. The approach not only provides insight and understanding into how thinking and feeling have an impact on behaviour, but also suggests practical strategies that counsellors can integrate into their counselling practice when working alongside their young clients to effect change.

This chapter begins by identifying the key principles of CBT and goes on to explore how the approach can inform counselling practice with young people. CBT strategies and techniques are introduced and you will have the opportunity to reflect on how these might be integrated into your own counselling practice with young people.

THE PRINCIPLES OF CBT

CBT emerged as a gradual integration of two schools of therapeutic thought:

- behavioural approaches;
- cognitive therapy.

Behavioural thinking (Watson, 1919; Pavlov, 1927; Skinner, 1953; Wolpe, 1958; Seligman, 1975) was born out of scientific enquiry into behaviour, in particular how a specific stimulus (something that happens) is likely to influence a response (what the individual does as a result). Behaviourists were scientists first and foremost, who believed that all behaviour is learned as a result of responses to stimuli and that it can therefore be 'un-learned' or changed. Claringbull sums up behaviourist thinking:

> *At birth we are blank slates (tabulae rasae) and life events engrave each of our individual personality patterns into each of our slates. For example, you might have had lots of belittling experiences in your life and so you have learned to be an introvert. Someone else has encountered nothing but praise and admiration and so has learned to be an extrovert.*
>
> (2010, p70)

Cognitive approaches, by contrast (Kelly, 1955; Beck, 1976; Bandura, 1977; Ellis 1989), suggest that *thinking* is central to how we behave. For example, if we have been burned by touching an electric fire, behaviourists would suggest that we learn, by stimulus and response, not to touch it again. However, our thinking (cognition) tells us that if the fire is turned off, then it poses no threat. Furthermore, our cognitive processes enable us to make a judgement about whether or not to touch the fire, based on an analysis of how recently it has been turned off and what risk it might still pose.

The cognitive theorists listed above, and Beck and Ellis in particular, cited the importance of unhelpful 'automatic thoughts' or 'irrational beliefs' which they suggested were grounded in messages received throughout an individual's life, but particularly in childhood. These 'negative automatic thoughts' (NATs) (Simmons and Griffiths, 2009) and irrational beliefs, are likely to influence behaviour, often in an unhelpful and restrictive way. Cognitive therapists emphasise the need to reduce and ultimately eliminate NATs and replace them with more rational, positive thinking.

In summary, CBT encompasses a broad amalgamation of both schools of therapy. It recognises that particular stimuli are likely to illicit behavioural responses, but it acknowledges that thoughts, beliefs and feelings play a significant part in influencing how we might behave in certain situations. Simply put, it is the relationship between thoughts, feelings and behaviour that forms the basis of CBT today.

McLeod summarises the approach neatly:

> *This approach has evolved out of behavioural psychology and has three key features: a problem-solving, change-focused approach to working with clients; a respect for scientific values; and close attention to the cognitive processes through which people monitor and control their behaviour.*
>
> (1998, p62)

If, as already stated, CBT focuses on *thoughts, beliefs* and *feelings* in order to understand, manage or change *behaviour,* then what are the underpinning principles of the approach? Who might benefit? And how effectively can counsellors integrate CBT techniques into their counselling practice? To begin, it is important to establish the key features of CBT. The approach:

- focuses on working towards change; change in thoughts, feelings – emotional and physical – and behaviour;
- involves exploring and challenging clients' thoughts and feelings – in particular their NATs and irrational beliefs;
- attends to the link between thoughts, feelings and behaviour;
- recognises that it is the client who is responsible for their actions and the counselling relationship is one of collaboration – 'working together';
- requires that clients (if not at first, then over time) recognise the need to change and become an active participant in the therapy;
- accesses a range of methods and techniques to enable change;
- engages the client in the process even when they are not with the counsellor (for example, techniques could include 'homework' tasks which clients undertake between sessions);
- states the goals of the therapy clearly and explicitly;
- is usually time-bound.

In the following counsellor testimony, Kai, an integrative counsellor who uses CBT techniques, describes how his knowledge of CBT informs his work with young people.

Practitioner reflections: Kai, a school counsellor, explains how CBT can inform practice

I work as an integrative counsellor in a school, which means that I draw on my knowledge of a range of counselling approaches and perspectives to inform my practice. CBT is one of the approaches I find myself considering frequently.

Many young people in school present with challenging or limiting behaviours. Whenever I see a young person whose behaviour is a cause for concern (for example, someone suffering panic attacks, lashing out at others, self-harming, losing weight, unable to manage their anger, and so on), I immediately think – CBT. I ensure that I work with the young person to explore the thoughts and feelings which may be influencing the behaviour. Often, in my experience, young people express limiting beliefs, thoughts, assumptions and feelings which are not necessarily based in reality and require challenging.

For example, I'm working with Kevin, a young lad who constantly tells me that he's 'rubbish', and he's 'thick'. Although there is no evidence to support these beliefs, the result of feeling this way is that Kevin avoids school at all costs, truants, runs out of lessons and so on. The consequence is that he doesn't do as well as he could in exams and is constantly behind in his work, missing vital stuff in lessons that he then doesn't understand. In other words, his beliefs, irrational as they might seem, have a profound impact on his behaviour. What we're doing in counselling is using CBT techniques to explore Kevin's beliefs about himself, consider where these come from and identify any evidence he has to support them. Then we will work to try to change the way Kevin sees himself; to reframe his thinking, I suppose. At first Kevin didn't see the point of counselling, but as the weeks have gone by, he has started to become much more engaged in the process. He seems to enjoy the active 'let's do something' nature of the approach, as do many young people, in my experience.

COMMENT

Kai explains that it is the presence of challenging and unwanted behaviours that alerts him to draw on his knowledge of CBT theory and strategies. Where there is an unwanted behaviour, this will generally be influenced by NATs (negative automatic thoughts) and irrational beliefs. Where NATs or irrational beliefs are challenged and changed, then behaviour should follow suit.

Of course, NATs and irrational beliefs are deeply held and have been learned over years as a response to a stimulus received (when working with young people this stimulus is likely to centre on messages from parental or authority figures). We have each heard and internalised messages received throughout our lives. Some of these may be positive, for example 'isn't

Jenny a clever little girl?' and some may be negative 'why do you always say the wrong thing at the wrong time? Be quiet!' It is not easy to change the way we see ourselves and to alter the deep-rooted beliefs we hold, based on messages that have been received and reinforced throughout our life. CBT requires young people to do just that (Trower et al. 2011). Furthermore, Geldard and Geldard (2009) make the point that young people often find the concept of 'irrational beliefs' unhelpful and will argue that their beliefs are perfectly rational. They therefore suggest the term 'self-destructive' beliefs which young people generally accept as making more sense.

REFLECTION POINT

- Reflect for a moment on some of the beliefs you hold about yourself. How would you describe yourself? Identify specific ways in which the significant messages you received in childhood still have an impact on your behaviour now.

We all hold irrational or self-destructive beliefs and NATs, which most of us manage and are able to identify for what they are. This is not to say that they do not still have an impact – they do. But in most cases we are able to minimise any potential negative influence and not let our behaviour become self-defeating, limiting or debilitating as a result.

CBT can be a helpful approach for those who are *unable* to *recognise* or *challenge* their own self-destructive beliefs, thoughts and feelings. These beliefs, thoughts and feelings have a negative influence on their behaviour and the way in which they live their lives.

Simmons and Griffiths (2009) provide a useful description of how self-destructive beliefs are developed. They use the analogy of 'shapes': squares for negative messages and stars for positive messages received in and after childhood. They explain that a person's square-shaped filter will become increasingly rigid as more and more negative (square-shaped) messages are received. In time, the square-shaped filter may become so fixed that it simply will not recognise or be flexible enough to 'let in' positive (star-shaped) messages. Thus, the negative messages are constantly reinforced and become internalised while the positive messages are simply not heard.

REFLECTION POINT

- What is your response to CBT so far? Think about clients you have worked with (or people you know – friends, family and colleagues) who hold what seem to you to be self-destructive or negative thoughts or beliefs about themselves.
- How have these thoughts/beliefs influenced their behaviour?

Geldard and Geldard (2004) assert that self-destructive beliefs fit into the following categories.

- Should, must, ought-to and have-to beliefs – 'I must be friends with Jim. After all, everyone likes him and then they'll like me too.'
- Catastrophising beliefs – 'If I get involved it is bound to go wrong.'
- 'Always' and 'never' beliefs – 'I always get off my head when I go out at the weekend, but it never has any negative effect.'
- Intolerance-of-others' beliefs – 'My teachers are talking rubbish when they say I could do really well.'
- Blaming beliefs – 'It's not my fault that I'm always getting caught shoplifting. My friends make me do it.'
- Negative self-perception beliefs – 'I feel so fat and ugly compared to my mates. I wish I could be one of the popular people.'

If we can recognise one or more of these categories of irrational thoughts in ourselves or others (to a greater or lesser extent), then we can be clear that all individuals are likely to hold some self-destructive thoughts and beliefs. CBT suggests that it is these unhelpful and limiting thoughts which are likely to impact in a negative way, on behaviour. Over the page is an example of how each 'category' of belief might influence behaviour (see Table 6.1).

Of course, it would be incorrect to say that each of the self-destructive beliefs listed overleaf will inevitably lead to the behavioural consequences detailed alongside. These are simply examples. That said, self-destructive beliefs are so named because that is what they are – self-destructive. In most cases the presence of these beliefs is likely to have a negative effect on the life of the young person.

Self-destructive belief	Possible behavioural consequences
Should, must, ought to, have to I *must* do well at school, I should pass all my exams with A grades. My parents *should* let me do what I want, like my friend's parents do. I *ought* to be as thin as the celebrities in the magazines.	*Should, must, ought to, have to.* Working too hard, panic attacks, stress-related behaviours or dropping out. Rebellion! Arguments and fights with parents and family. Lack of self-esteem, unhealthy eating, ultimately risk of eating disorders.
Catastrophising If I don't go to that party/smoke that joint/steal that handbag everyone will hate me. My boyfriend has dumped me. How can I ever face my friends again? There's no point in going for that job, I'll never get it.	*Catastrophising* Risk-taking or dangerous behaviour 'going along with the crowd'. Telling lies, trivialising, putting on a 'brave face' in front of friends. Choosing not to take action because it's bound to fail.
Always and never I'm *always* rubbish at maths. There's no point even trying. There's no part in asking my dad if I can go. He *never* says yes to anything. It's *always* my fault when things go wrong.	*Always and never* Never taking risks, under-performing, accepting failure is inevitable. Refusing to ask, difficulty in hearing negative responses, fear of failure. Fatalistic, passive, aggressive behaviour.
Intolerance of others' beliefs My sister always does that, just to spite me. That's the second time my friend has forgotten we're going out. She does it on purpose. Why can't he get drunk like the rest of us? He's so boring!	*Intolerance of others' beliefs* Aggressive, negative feelings towards sister. Damaging relationship with friend, expressing anger, feeling hurt and unloved. Intolerance. Possibly losing a friendship which might have been a positive one.

Table 6.1: How beliefs may impact on behaviour

Self-destructive belief	Possible behavioural consequences
Blaming beliefs I can't go out, my mum won't let me. It's not fair. My sister gets all of the attention. No one's bothered about me. My friends keep getting me into trouble at school, it's always them, never me.	*Blaming beliefs* Inaction. Someone else is the 'bad guy'. Reinforces negative feelings, depression, passivity or attention-seeking behaviour. Unhelpful behaviour continues. No change necessary! It wasn't 'my fault' in the first place.
Negative self-perception beliefs I'm rubbish. I'm stupid. I'm fat. I'm ugly. I'm bad. I'm unlovable.	*Negative self-perception beliefs* In each of the examples the young person might 'act out' or 'live up' to their belief, reinforcing the belief through their behaviour. They are likely to feel unhappy, unpopular and unlikeable.

Table 6.1: How beliefs may impact on behaviour (continued)

ACTIVITY 6.1

- Identify a client with whom you have worked who has expressed a self-destructive belief (refer to the list above). Try to make links between the belief and the behaviour (in other words, what impact did this belief have on the young person's behaviour?).
- How did you work with this in counselling? This is something that you might want to explore further in supervision.

To recognise that we all hold NATs and irrational or self-destructive beliefs is one thing. To challenge and adapt these thoughts and beliefs in order to effect changes in behaviour is another. Geldard and Geldard suggest alternative *constructive* beliefs which the counsellor can assist the young person to consider, explore and ultimately use to replace the negative, thereby reframing their thinking. But they advise caution: self-destructive beliefs are embedded; they are a part of who we are. Giving them up and replacing them with something different (in other words, changing the way in which we think) can be a daunting, anxiety-raising business.

So, how do we do it? One of the attractions of CBT to both counsellors and clients is that it is a proactive and often practical therapeutic approach. Counsellors have access to a number of strategies and techniques which they can use with clients during counselling and, in turn, clients collaborate in tasks and learn techniques that they then use outside of the counselling room. In other words, clients put their learning into practice as part of their everyday lives. For young people, this proactive and essentially energising and collaborative approach can be engaging and positive. It feels as though they are *doing* something. Research supports the use of CBT techniques with young people, particularly when dealing with issues such as depression, anxiety, lack of motivation, anger management and difficulties with integration (Valliant and Antonowicz, 1991; Geldard and Geldard, 2009).

If we accept that CBT offers counsellors a way of understanding how young people's thoughts, beliefs and feelings impact on their behaviour (particularly in an unhelpful and self-destructive way), what strategies and methods can counsellors use that will help to engender change?

USING CBT TECHNIQUES IN COUNSELLING PRACTICE

There is a plethora of CBT techniques which have been developed in order to address two distinct elements:

1   to challenge and change *cognitions;*
2   to manage *behaviour.*

Of course, one of the key principles of CBT is that thoughts, beliefs and feelings influence behaviour. Therefore, by challenging the NATs, self-destructive beliefs and emotional content of what a client brings to counselling and encouraging clients to adjust their thinking, changes in behaviour should, over time, take place. However, there are also CBT techniques which focus specifically on behaviour. These behavioural techniques offer clients the opportunity to manage their behaviour more effectively while they are working to understand, challenge and adapt the underpinning limiting thoughts and feelings.

There is not scope here to provide a full and detailed analysis of the many and various techniques which are regularly used by CBT counsellors (see, for example, Greenberger and Padesky, 1995; Leahy, 2003; Sanders and Wills, 2005; Wills, 2008; Simmons and Griffiths, 2009). Instead, some key techniques and strategies are offered and introduced under the headings *cognitive* and *behavioural techniques* and examples of how these may be used when counselling young people. Through this section (as is the case throughout this book) it is helpful to reflect on client work, to consider young people you have worked with in counselling and to evaluate when, if at all, one or more of these strategies may have been useful. As with any introduction to a particular counselling approach and techniques, it is important to offer a 'health warning'. Counsellors should be aware of the dangers of 'trying out' a technique simply because counselling feels 'stuck' and no progress appears to be taking place. A full analysis and assessment of the client and their presenting problem is essential in order to decide whether or not a chosen approach is appropriate to integrate into the work. Most importantly, the therapeutic alliance, referred to throughout this book, should be firmly in place before any decisions are made about possible approaches to use with clients. Wills expresses this point succinctly:

> *CBT is a skill oriented form of therapy but its skills need to be firmly based on a set of principles governing how to understand client problems and to help in the planning and execution of interventions to ameliorate such problems.*

(2008, p13)

COGNITIVE TECHNIQUES

There is a range of techniques that counsellors can use in order to help young people challenge their NATs and self-destructive beliefs. Two are listed below and are described, in brief:

- challenging and reframing thinking;
- thought recording.

Challenging and reframing thinking

When young people express negative automatic thoughts and self-destructive beliefs (as they often do), the role of the counsellor is to enable the client to challenge these unhelpful thoughts and reframe their thinking. For example, it is probably not effective to tell a young person who thinks that they are unattractive or unpopular, that they are not. Simply disagreeing is unlikely to help, as the young person will 'filter out' and disregard any positive feedback from the counsellor. But gentle questioning, asking the client to support their thinking with evidence and focusing on occasions in their lives where they have not felt this way, will help to challenge and reframe the young person's thinking. The 'what is the worst that might happen?' question is also a good way of encouraging young people to think more realistically and engage in a conversation about their thoughts and beliefs. The table below, shown earlier in the chapter, suggests some possible responses to young people's self-destructive beliefs, which might act as a *starting point* to greater exploration.

Self-destructive belief	Possible response
Should, must, ought to, have to I *must* do well at school, I should pass all my exams with A grades.	*Should, must, ought to, have to* Who is telling you that you must achieve these grades at all costs?
My parents *should* let me do what I want like my friend's parents do.	What makes you think they don't let you do what you want?
I *ought* to be as thin as the celebrities in the magazines.	And how would your life be different if you *were* very thin like those celebrities?
Catastrophising If I don't go to that party/smoke that joint/steal that handbag everyone will hate me.	*Catastrophising* What is the worst that can happen if you say 'no' to that party/joint/stealing?
My boyfriend has dumped me. How can I ever face my friends again?	What is the worst that can happen when you tell your friends?
There's no point in going for that job, I'll never get it.	I wonder why you say that. What evidence do you have that you won't get the job?
Always and never I'm *always* rubbish at maths. There's no point even trying.	*Always and never* It's hard when we don't feel we're good at things. What will happen if you continue not to try?
There's no part in asking my dad if I can go. He *never* says yes to anything.	Can you think of a time when your dad *has* agreed to something you wanted to do?
It's *always* my fault when things go wrong, *never* anyone else's.	Tell me about a time when something went wrong and it wasn't your fault.
Intolerance of others' beliefs My sister always does that. She does it on purpose, just to spite me.	*Intolerance of others' beliefs* What evidence do you have that your sister wants to spite you?
That's the second time my friend has forgotten we're going out. She does it on purpose.	There are times when we all forget things. What evidence is there that she's done it on purpose?

Table 6.2: Self-destructive beliefs and possible responses

Self-destructive belief	Possible response
Why can't he get drunk like the rest of us? He's so boring!	How important is this friend to you? What might happen if you told him that he's boring?
Blaming beliefs I can't go out, my mum won't let me.	*Blaming beliefs* How would you feel if your mum *would* let you?
It's not fair. My sister gets all of the attention. No one's bothered about me.	What makes you say that? Tell me about times when people have shown that they *are* bothered.
My friends keep getting me into trouble at school; it's always them, never me.	If a friend came to you with this problem, what would you suggest they do?
Negative self-perception beliefs I'm rubbish. I'm stupid. I'm fat. I'm ugly. I'm bad. I'm unlovable.	*Negative self-perception beliefs* Asking for evidence to support the negative self-perception is often a helpful starting point. Encouraging young people to consider any exceptions to these times when they haven't felt this way about themselves and focus on exploring these.

Table 6.2: Self-destructive beliefs and possible responses (continued)

REFLECTION POINT

- What are your initial thoughts about the suggested responses to self-destructive beliefs detailed above? Can you think of ways in which you have responded to clients who hold self-destructive beliefs?
- How effective have your challenges been? Consider and write down suggestions for alternative responses.

By challenging thoughts, feelings and beliefs (particularly those that are negative or self-destructive), young people can begin to understand their behaviour better and seek to make changes. The suggestions above simply offer a starting point from which exploration, challenge and reflection can develop. Wills makes a helpful comment about challenging negative thoughts and beliefs:

> *Sometimes merely identifying negative thinking in itself, without conscious modification, can set off a process of change.*
>
> (2008, p57)

Thought recording

There are various examples of thought records or diaries that can be used to encourage clients to identify the specific times that their NATs or self-destructive beliefs have an impact on their behaviour (Ellis, 2001; Dryden, 2005; Sanders and Wills, 2005; Wills, 2008; Simmons and Griffiths, 2009). It is often difficult for young people to recall in detail examples of situations where their thoughts had a negative effect on their feelings or behaviour. By keeping a record of the occasions when they experienced negative thoughts or self-destructive beliefs, young people can begin to recognise the 'triggers' or circumstances in which these unhelpful thoughts are manifest. This can be enlightening. The thought records may be brought to counselling and act as a useful starting point for discussion. Thought records can be tailored, adapted or simplified. Normally, the headings in Table 6.3 should be included.

What is recorded here is a detailed account of an event that took place and the resulting emotions, thoughts, physical responses and consequences experienced by the young person. This provides rich material for counselling, but, as importantly, it offers the client a tool for reflection and a way of naming and expressing their thoughts on a regular basis. By undertaking this activity, following significant events, the young person is provided with the opportunity to reflect on what happened and, over time, to analyse patterns, recognise triggers or 'risky' situations, and work towards changing the way they think and respond.

REFLECTION POINT

- Can you think of clients for whom keeping a thought record might be a useful activity? How might it help?
- What might be the barriers to completing such a record? How could you encourage your client to overcome those barriers?

COMMENT

For some young people, expressing themselves in writing may prove a barrier to completing a thought record. They may find that the task has negative connotations associated with 'homework'. It might be that some young people would rather express themselves in other ways. This is not a problem. The thought record could be completed in a number of creative ways – perhaps in pictorial form, composing images or pictures which represent the

Date and time	Situation	Feelings	Thoughts	Body changes	Behaviour
When did this happen?	What were you doing at the time? Who were you with? What was going on around you?	Describe your emotions at the time and try to recall the intensity of the emotions, perhaps by 'scaling' them 1–10 (where 1 = not intense at all, and 10 = very intense)	Identify what you were thinking at the time. What is the strength of that thought? Again, you might like to use a 'scale' of 1–10	Were there any changes in your body at the time? For example, did your heart beat quicken, palms sweat, experience faster breathing, tension in shoulders?	What did you actually do as a result of the thoughts/feelings that you were experiencing?
Saturday, 9pm	I was at a party. It looked like my mate was flirting with my girlfriend. He asked my girlfriend to dance with him.	Angry with my mate = 9 Worried that my girlfriend would rather be with him than me = 8	I knew he'd try to steal my girlfriend = 9 She'll dump me = 8 This always happens to me. Just when I think things are going well, it all goes wrong =10	My hands clenched. I got hot and I couldn't breathe properly. I saw red.	I faced up to my mate and told him to 'back off'. I wanted to hit him but some of my other mates pulled me off. I got chucked out of the club.

Table 6.3: Thought recording

thoughts, feelings and behaviours. Alternatively, clients could write lyrics or identify pieces of music that express their thoughts and feelings. Like all of the techniques suggested in this chapter, they will only be helpful if the client can be encouraged to value and 'buy into' the experience.

BEHAVIOURAL TECHNIQUES

The techniques and strategies introduced so far focus specifically on addressing negative thoughts and self-destructive beliefs. They are con- cerned with the *cognitive* element of cognitive behavioural therapy. In addition, there is a range of techniques which can be used in order to manage and change unhelpful or limiting *behaviours*. Two of these strategies are discussed here:

- goal setting;
- ABC technique.

Goal setting

At certain times we may find ourselves identifying changes that we would like to make in our lives. These changes are most likely to take place if we set specific aims or goals. The technique of goal setting in CBT recognises the importance of:

- identifying a specific behaviour that is unhelpful;
- reflecting on when/how the behaviour occurs;
- setting goals for change.

The counsellor will work with the young person to ensure that the goals are:

- SMART (specific, measureable, achievable, realistic, time-bound);
- the client's own.

The case study below shows **Claire**, a school counsellor, working with **Stacey**, a 14-year-old pupil who has an eating disorder.

Case study 6.1   Goal setting in counselling

Claire: 'So it sounds as though things haven't been great this week, Stacey. Looking at your "thought diary", it seems you've made yourself sick at least once every day. Is that right?'

Stacey: 'Yeah. I know. It's awful. I hate it, I hate myself, but I love how it makes me feel at the same time. But I really, really do want to change.'

Claire: 'Yes, I can hear that. I know that we've discussed your feelings about what's going on and it's important that we continue to do that. What I'm also thinking is that we might want to consider setting some really practical aims. What I mean by that is to think about what you can realistically change by setting a goal for yourself.'

Stacey: 'Umm . . .I don't understand . . .'

Claire: 'Well, for example, you could consider reducing the number of times each day that you make yourself sick. It looks from your diary as though your most difficult time is when you get home from school and binge on biscuits and sweets. On the other hand, you don't always make yourself sick after breakfast or lunch. So, how about if you try eating your breakfast this week without throwing up afterwards? How would that feel?'

Stacey: 'Scary!'

Claire: 'OK, scary,' (pause) 'but possible?'

Stacey: 'Yeah, maybe. I could give it a try. It's true that evenings are more difficult for me, so breakfast is probably the best time to start. Also, it's more difficult in the mornings because my mum's around and she's listening out for how much time I spend in the bathroom, (pause) yeah, OK. I'll give it a go.'

Claire: 'Well, how about if we write your goal down on your thought diary for this week. Then next time we meet up we can look at how well you've done?'

Stacey: 'Good idea. It still feels scary though. I don't know if it's possible. Maybe. I hope so. (Pause) I'm going to give it a go. Who knows, this time next week I might even have got by without being sick after breakfast once!'

Claire: 'That would be great. And then we could look at making sure we continue to meet that goal and maybe think about others too, like not being sick after lunch.'

COMMENT

Of course, there is no guarantee that Stacey will achieve her goal and much exploration of thoughts and feelings should accompany this practical, behavioural strategy. But, as with all CBT techniques, this is a starting point; a possible way forward for Stacey that will help her to achieve and feel positive about how effectively she is managing this debilitating behaviour; while continuing to address her underlying negative automatic thoughts and self-defeating beliefs in the counselling room.

ACTIVITY 6.2

- Discuss with a friend/colleague times in your own life when you have set goals for yourself. Explain what has helped you to achieve these goals? What has stopped you? Finally, identify a personal goal that you would like to set for the future.

COMMENT

It is important to recognise that goal setting is only effective if there is commitment. If a young person does not have a desire to change their behaviour, then the activity of goal setting is bound to fail. Goals should be SMART and should, if possible, be recorded. It is important too that progression towards goals is discussed during counselling. It may be, if goals are not achieved, smaller sub-goals are identified. The positive experience of meeting goals should not be underestimated. The young person will recognise and 'own' their achievement, realising that change is possible and that they have the power to make it happen.

ABC technique

The ABC technique (Ellis, 1962; Trower et al., 2011) encourages the client to recognise the triggers and beliefs that could ultimately lead to negative consequences. ABC stands for the following:

A = Activating event
B = Belief
C = Consequences

Sheldon (1995) and Wills (2008) adapt the language and therefore adjust slightly the emphasis of the ABC approach. Here ABC refers to:

A = Antecedents (triggers for the behaviour, including situations, thoughts and beliefs)
B = Behaviour (the resulting behaviour, i.e. what actually happens?)
C = Consequences (the after-effects of the behaviour)

When focusing on the *antecedents*, young people can acknowledge (and try to avoid) the situations, thoughts and beliefs that trigger unhelpful *behaviour*, because they are aware of the possible negative *consequences* that may ensue. In the example below, this ABC technique is used to analyse the antecedents and consequences of Carl's behaviour. Carl is an 18-year-old, who has recently been arrested for violent conduct.

Case study 6.2   Carl

Carl has been involved in fights throughout his life. He can remember, as far back as primary school, being in trouble for violence towards other children. In recent years, the situation has become exacerbated and Carl has been arrested on a number of occasions for violent conduct and assault. Carl describes a pattern whereby the following antecedents (A), trigger his violent behaviour:

- alcohol;
- drugs;
- being in situations with large groups (clubs, pubs, parties).

The violent behaviour (B) often begins as a 'stand-off' where Carl thinks that someone else is 'looking at me'. This escalates into a verbal exchange, followed by abuse and finally Carl throws the first punch. Once he is involved in a physical fight, he loses control and the ability to do anything other than batter his opponent.

What happens as a consequence (C) is that Carl inflicts damage on another (often innocent) individual and puts himself at risk of injury in return. He is often in trouble with the police and he has lost a number of friends who don't like to be around him when he gets like this.

ACTIVITY 6.3

- Discuss with a colleague how you might use the ABC approach with Carl in order to assist him to manage his behaviour better. What strategies might he identify at the antecedent stage that could limit the destructive behaviour?

Using the ABC approach as a way to understand and adapt behaviour can be both practical and illuminating. Counsellors who adopt this technique often write the headings Antecedent, Behaviour and Consequence on a grid which they use with clients in counselling. The aim is to understand the triggers and consequences, and ensure that situations where the antecedent is likely to occur are reduced. In Carl's case, this may mean helping him to explore ways in which he can avoid or minimise the triggers of alcohol, drugs and being around large groups in social situations, thereby reducing the risk of the violent behaviour and its consequences.

CHAPTER SUMMARY

This chapter introduces the key principles of CBT; the acknowledgement that our thoughts, feelings and beliefs (and in particular our NATs and self-destructive beliefs) may have an impact on our behaviour. Where this behaviour is unwanted, negative or harmful, then the CBT techniques and strategies offered here may provide the counsellor with a way forward in helping young people to understand themselves better and to effect change where they can.

It is important to stress that CBT offers neither a magic wand nor a sure-fire strategy for success. Some young people may respond positively to the techniques, others may not. But as part of an integrative approach to counselling, where unwanted behaviours are evident and self-defeating beliefs are aired, then the counsellor's awareness of CBT might act as a useful starting point for the work.

SUGGESTED FURTHER READING

Sanders, D and Wills, F (2005) *Cognitive Therapy: An Introduction.* London: Sage.

An excellent resource which engages the reader and presents the key principles of the approach in a helpful way.

Simmons, J and Griffiths, R (2009) *CBT for Beginners.* London: Sage.

A great introduction to CBT. In particular, part 2 of the book which focuses on 'how do you do it?'.

Trower, P, Jones, J, Dryden, W and Casey, A (2011) *Cognitive Behavioural Counselling in Action*, 2nd edition. London: Sage.

As always, the 'in action' series does not disappoint, providing the reader with a clear and helpful insight into CBT.

Wills, F (2008) *Cognitive Behaviour Counselling and Psychotherapy.* London: Sage.

Another very accessible and readable text, with plenty of practice examples to stimulate thinking.

Wilson, R and Branch, R (2006) *Cognitive Behavioural Therapy for Dummies.* Chichester: Wiley.

A text much praised by those who are embarking on cognitive behavioural training.

CHAPTER 7

Using motivational interviewing to engage young people in timely interventions

by Hazel Reid

CORE KNOWLEDGE

By the end of this chapter you will have the opportunity to:

- gain an overview of motivational interviewing;
- identify the general principles of motivational interviewing;
- explore aspects of the approach that could be applied to your practice;
- consider the usefulness of the concept of the 'wheel of change' as a diagnostic tool.

INTRODUCTION

Motivational interviewing is concerned with change and people's resistance to change. In life, as well as in counselling, we often wonder why people in circumstances that are clearly causing them harm continue with their destructive behaviour. Why do intelligent beings continue to overeat when they know that obesity can lead to health problems and a reduced life expectancy – ditto smoking, alcoholism, or substance misuse? Why continue in an abusive relationship or abuse others when the outcomes are felt as negative and damaging leading to psychological and often physical injury? And why is the pattern of behaviour not broken when the individual is receiving help from others, including professional help? Resistance to change in a counselling relationship can be significantly influenced by the style of the counsellor. 'Counsel in a directive, confrontational manner, and client resistance goes up. Counsel in a reflective, supportive manner, and resistance goes down while change talk increases' (Miller and Rollnick, 2002).

Paying attention to what people *say* in a counselling interview (change talk), alongside how they say it, being supportive and empathic, avoiding simple 'advice giving' – all would be cornerstones of most counselling approaches, so what does motivational counselling offer that is different? In motivational interviewing the phenomenon of *ambivalence* is explored (in simple terms, 'being in two minds'); and its effects on decision making and avoidance, alongside the concept of *readiness* for change. The conditions for change are positioned in a social and cultural context experienced by the individual. Others, including counsellors, who are not living the 'problem', should avoid making assumptions about the effects of the issue on the individual and the degree of importance they place on the perceived problem. Thus, rather than ask why the person is not motivated to stop overeating, give up smoking and so on, the question becomes, 'What *is* this person motivated to do?'. Finding out what motivates an individual can be the start of working towards a process of change that is valued by that individual; rather than a change process that is over-influenced by the counsellor's values.

The approach also aims to address any perceived limiting beliefs about issues that create barriers to moving towards action. With many young people the 'usual' teenage difficulties around conflicting emotions, lack of confidence, low self-esteem and motivation require the counsellor to be sensitive to these limiting beliefs. Motivational interviewing aims to explore and address the 'stuckness' that young people experience that makes moving forward difficult – at the current time, in their current context. In addition, through exploring the 'wheel of change' as a diagnostic tool, counsellors can also reflect further on what it is they are doing that may be hindering motivation for change.

A CONSTRUCTIVIST FRAMEWORK

Motivational interviewing sits within a constructivist framework, so, before going further, it is important to explore the meaning of 'constructivist' in terms of youth counselling. A brief review will provide a background for this and the following chapters. Social constructionism was discussed in the chapter on multiculturalism, where it was explained that constructivist approaches move away from a positivist ideology by placing individual meaning, respectfully, in the foreground. The intention of all constructivist approaches is to explore notions of identity, in the broadest life-wide sense, encompassing personal values and motivators, desire and resistance: in relation to new opportunities and change, where change is sought. This can be described as moving away from twentieth-century models rooted in scientific discovery, 'facts' and explanations (positivist), to twenty-first-century approaches based on understanding 'meanings' (constructivist). The latter are viewed as being more congruent with the way people live and learn in contemporary society.

REFLECTION POINT

- What were the social and economic conditions in the West that gave rise to early twentieth-century models in psychology being described as 'positivist'?
- Take a little time thinking about what was going on at the time in terms of the development of psychology as a social 'science'. Why was it called a science? How had ideas changed about 'man's' relation to nature, to God and to processes of production and industry?
- What were the 'big' theories at the time – sometimes referred to as 'grand narratives'? McLeod (2009) will be an informative read here.

WHAT IS MOTIVATIONAL INTERVIEWING?

Motivational interviewing, as developed by William Miller and Stephen Rollnick, is now well recognised in the areas of substance abuse counselling, healthcare, social work and youth justice; and evident in fields such as educational welfare, career and youth counselling (Beven, 2009). Miller and Rollnick do not appear to use the term 'motivational counselling', as they describe the approach as a method of communicating with clients, rather than a therapeutic intervention. That said they do refer to the practitioner as a 'counsellor'. In addition, the principles and activities can be applied in a wide range of settings, which may or may not involve counselling. For example, a clinician could use the approach when guiding a patient on improving their use of medical aids, devices and medicines. For instance, although it may improve mobility, a patient may be resistant to using a walking frame if that involves a behavioural change and view of self that they find unacceptable at the current time. 'Telling them' to do it will have little effect and often a negative outcome will be the result (the frame gets left in the spare bedroom). Advising a young person with a hearing impairment that wearing their hearing aid will help them to perform better in school will not make them wear it unless they can envisage and *want* the benefits that changing their behaviour will bring.

Miller and Rollnick (2002) define motivational interviewing as both directive and client-centred. It aims to generate behavioural change by helping clients to explore and resolve areas in their thinking about the future that they are ambivalent or indecisive about. The outcome for behavioural change makes the approach appear more focused and goal-directed than many counselling models. For this reason it may appeal to those counselling young people as there is often a sense of urgency for them (the young person) to make progress more rapidly. Thus, goal-directed approaches, such as motivational interviewing, can be helpful where young people are 'stuck' and finding it difficult to move forward, or where there are many problems or issues to be resolved. However, using the word 'directive' can be disconcerting when employed alongside 'client-centred', but directive here means working toward behavioural change – not telling the client what to do. What is referred to as the 'spirit of motivational interviewing' (Miller and Rollnick, 2002, p35) pays close attention to counselling processes. Motivational interviewing is informed by key components such as working collaboratively and alongside the client, not taking an expert role, but evoking – or drawing out – the motivation for change that is within the person; and acting at all times to foster client autonomy in decision making:

> *When motivational interviewing is done properly, it is the client rather than the counsellor who presents the arguments for change.*
> (Miller and Rollnick, 2002, p34)

As with all the approaches in this book, there is a risk that harvesting techniques for an integrated model for counselling will dilute the fundamental principles that underpin the thinking behind motivational interviewing – leading to not doing it properly. These principles are discussed in the next section, before moving on to look at activities that can be explored further for counselling work with young people. But first it may be useful to offer a definition of motivation. Miller and Rollnick (2002) define motivation as a state of readiness to take action. Beven adds:

> *We need to move away from stereotypical notions of individuals either being motivated or not motivated. It seems evident that motivation is always context specific, is changeable over time – sometimes quite a short period of time, and is influenced by perceived power relationships.*
> (2009, p13)

REFLECTION POINT

- Think about a time when you have been very motivated to engage in an activity that brought about changed behaviour – what was the context, the time frame and how in control did you feel? What about a time when you were not motivated to undertake the same activity – what were the circumstances that influenced you then? So, how did the timing of the experience, context and relationships with others influence your motivation?

GENERAL PRINCIPLES

Rollnick and Miller (1995) identified behaviours in the practitioner that are characteristic of a motivational interviewing approach. The core values and skills underpinning these behaviours are evident in other counselling approaches and are:

- seeking to understand the young person's frame of reference: their world view, particularly through the skills of reflective listening;
- expressing acceptance and affirmation, demonstrating unconditional positive regard (Rogers, 1951);
- eliciting and selectively reinforcing the young person's own self-motivational statements, expressions of problem recognition, concern, desire and intention to change, and the ability to change;
- monitoring the young person's degree of readiness to change, and ensuring that resistance is not generated by moving forward too quickly (i.e. jumping ahead of the young person);
- affirming the young person's freedom of choice and self-direction.

In a later refinement of the approach, Miller and Rollnick (2002, p36) describe four general principles. These are:

- express empathy;
- develop discrepancy;
- roll with resistance;
- support self-efficacy.

1. Express empathy

Empathy is more than a skill: it is a way of being with the young person in counselling. It has already been discussed earlier in the book, but it is worth repeating that empathy is not a reaction that is switched on and off at an appropriate time (and there is something rather chilling in that notion). The crucial attitude required is one of acceptance and respectful listening, and curiosity in order to understand the young person's perspective. 'The attitude of acceptance and respect builds a working therapeutic alliance and supports the client's self-esteem, which further promotes change' (Miller and Rollnick, 2002, p37). An empathic counsellor accepts *ambivalence* (where opposite feelings co-exist alongside each other) as a normal part of human experience and response to change. Reluctance to change behaviour is a normal phenomenon in youth counselling, otherwise (if change had already occurred) the young person would not be in need of counselling.

The concept of ambivalence can be depicted using the metaphor of scales where the 'for and against' can be weighed against each other. However, this suggests a rational approach leading to a decision, but ambivalence indicates indecision or a see-sawing back and forwards between 'I do and I don't/ I want to and I don't want to'. Changing behaviour means giving something up and there are costs as well as benefits; even when what may be given up is something perceived as negative, it is a known way of being, whereas the new behaviour is unknown and therefore risky. An empathic counsellor understands the paradox of resistance to change and avoids thinking of young people as indecisive or poorly motivated. They recognise that the young person has not reached the point of *readiness* for change.

2. Develop discrepancy

Motivational interviewing is 'intentionally directive – directed toward the resolution of ambivalence in the service of change' (Miller and Rollnick, 2002, p38). It differs from client-centred work in that it is not designed to accept people the way they are. The aim is to change the young person's perception of the current situation. But the intention is that the client, not the counsellor, should present the arguments for change. Particularly when counselling young people who are well practised in ignoring 'advice', a statement regarding change is more persuasive when initiated by the young person themselves. The motivation for change arises when the young person can perceive a discrepancy between their present behaviour and their wider goals and values. This is not just about how much change is needed to accomplish the future goals, as if the gap between the two is large it becomes an abyss and is demotivating. It is about the young person identifying what is important to change in line with their goals and values, rather than in response to external pressure to conform to the goals of others. Motivation comes from the young person highlighting the discrepancy, but action for positive change needs to be timely, appropriate and staged. To clarify the above, consider the case study below in terms of discrepancy and ambivalence.

Case study 7.1   Ambivalence is a good thing!

Jon is a young dad who 'drinks too much'. His partner Donna wants him to help more with the toddler, Ben, but complains that Jon is too often 'off his head with booze', even in the daytime. Jon promises he'll not drink before lunchtime and says he will collect Ben from preschool at 12 o'clock. He leaves home on time, but meets a mate on the way who wants to talk to him. Jon explains he has to go, but says he'll meet his mate in half an hour and they can watch a DVD together and have a drink. Jon realises he'll have to get some cans and thinks he can get some from the supermarket before collecting Ben. It has started to rain and that makes him decide to get the cans now. Looking at the preschool entrance he sees the children coming out with their mums and dads, but thinks Ben will be OK for a minute, so rushes into the supermarket to buy the cans.

Jon tells this story to Val, the counsellor who is now working with Jon on his alcohol issues, and ends by saying: 'the preschool teacher was cross as she had seen me go in the supermarket, but it wasn't that so much as . . . well, afterwards I thought what kind of dad does that – puts buying cans of beer before picking up his four-year-old kid?'

COMMENT

Jon has not changed his view about drinking or his values regarding what constitutes being a good father, but it is the realisation that drinking has become more important than looking after Ben that has become unacceptable to him. The behaviour – drinking – has come into conflict with his deeply held value about being a dad. Jon is recognising the discrepancy between his behaviour and his values, and is, perhaps, becoming ambivalent about his drinking. Miller and Rollnick state that for many people 'the first step toward change is to *become* ambivalent' (2002, p23). In this way ambivalence, if it continues to grow, helps rather than hinders change.

In helping people to 'face the reality of their situation', 'resolve ambivalence' and work toward 'positive change', Miller and Rollnick acknowledge that there are ethical and value-laden overtones to such statements. However, in addition to offering guidelines for ethical practice, they emphasise that watchfulness with regard to the core values and principles avoids coerciveness; in other words, avoids applying strategies which override what the individual wants. Thus, the concepts of ambivalence and discrepancy work together to promote change. You cannot be ambivalent about change if there is no discrepancy between the present position and desired goals.

> *As discrepancy increases, ambivalence first intensifies; then, if the discrepancy continues to grow, ambivalence can be resolved in the direction of change.*
>
> (Miller and Rollnick, 2002, p23)

To facilitate change the counsellor who listens and attends without offering solutions can promote 'change talk'. A counsellor who listens and reflects back can encourage the young person to keep talking. Offering solutions on the other hand can lead to 'road blocks', halting the young person in their tracks, leading to resistance (Miller and Rollnick, 2002, p181). Useful questions in motivational interviewing that can also facilitate change and change talk (at the point of readiness) are as follows.

- What changes would you most like to talk about?
- What have you noticed about . . .?
- How important is it for you to change . . .?
- How confident do you feel about changing . . .?
- How do you see the benefits of . . .?
- How do you see the drawback of . . .?
- What will make the most sense to you?
- How might things be different if you . . .?
- In what way . . .?
- Where does this leave you now . . .?

(Rollnick et al., 2010, p7)

3. Roll with resistance

In line with what has been said earlier, when trying to evoke change it is counterproductive for the counsellor to push for change, suggest goals and propose action steps. This 'pushing' can be due to dissatisfaction when experiencing the young person's resistance, where the counsellor feels they are not being competent. Suggesting solutions, outlining options and offering action steps in what is meant to be a supportive and enthusiastic manner, will *feel* helpful to the counsellor (Beven, 2009). The likely reaction from the young person is merely to agree, but then to ignore the suggestions or to argue, defend and entrench their current position. Miller and Rollnick use the expression to 'roll with resistance' to clarify that, rather than get into confrontational positions, the practitioner rolls or flows with resistance instead of opposing resistance. In this way the responsibility for change is not taken on by the counsellor, it remains with the young person as the autonomous individual who is the expert on their own situation. And in any case, making suggestions quite often ends up in a resistance game (as in transactional analysis) of 'Ah, yes but . . .'. This does not mean that new perspectives on the issue cannot be sought, but these are not imposed, permission is sought to offer information on alternatives.

> *The counsellor does not impose new views or goals; rather, the person is invited to consider new information and is offered new perspectives. 'Take what you want and leave the rest' is the permissive kind of advice that pervades this approach.*
>
> (Miller and Rollnick, 2002, p40)

Recognising resistance is an important skill for the counsellor, as it also indicates that the current way of communicating is not working and a change is required. In this way resistance can be reframed as feedback from the young person, 'a reaction to some perceived threat' (Beven, 2009, p13). In addition, it can help to avoid a defensive positioning from the counsellor who may be thinking, if not saying, 'Nothing I suggest is taken seriously' or, if the young person does not engage and the session ends abruptly, 'Well, hopefully they'll come back when they do want to talk about something!' What is interesting in the last statement is that the young person may not have engaged, but they were communicating. Lack of engagement *is* communicating – feeding back – that the approach needs changing.

Resistant behaviour can be fed back through the young person:

- **arguing** with the accuracy of what is being said, being hostile or discounting what the counsellor says;
- **interrupting**, breaking into the conversation in a defensive manner or 'cutting off' the counsellor;
- **negating** that the problem exists, or being unwilling to cooperate, take responsibility or accept an invitation to consider information;

- **ignoring** the counsellor or not following the conversation (being present, but withdrawn).

Using the technique of 'pros and cons' can be a way of encouraging a young person to talk about change. The aim is to understand the young person's reluctance and encourage them to work towards making change statements. Rather than evaluating the 'for and against' of a new option, the process often begins by considering the current situation and asking the young person what they like about *not* changing; in other words, remaining as they are at present. This approach can reveal what the young person sees as the benefits of not changing, what they see as meaningful in staying the same. Moving on to the aspects that 'are not so good' in the current situation, encourages the young person to state and own the reasons for change. This fits with the autonomous approach where it is the young person, not the counsellor, who voices the reasons for change (Beven, 2009).

Case study 7.2   Abby

Abby has been referred to the school counsellor, Tilly, as she has started to self-harm. On her second visit Tilly wants to find out more about what self-harming means to Abby. Abby calls the behaviour, 'my cutting'.

Tilly: 'I want to understand your self-harming better from your point of view, both the benefits and what you see as the disadvantages. Can I ask you first what you like about your cutting – what are the benefits?'
Abby: 'When I get really stressed, it kind of releases that – makes me feel better for a bit.'
Tilly: 'Tell me a bit more, Abby, about how it releases the stress.'

Using respectful curiosity, Tilly asks further questions to elicit a good understanding.

Tilly: 'Now can I ask you about what you don't like about your cutting?'
Abby: 'Well it upsets my Mum and I have to keep my arms covered up so that people cannot see the cuts.'
Tilly: 'There are two things there, tell me first about what it means to you that it upsets your Mum.'
Tilly avoids offering her own perspective on self-harming as she wants Abby to talk about the experience and what it means to her. Abby is also encouraged to talk about what it means to have to cover up her arms so that others cannot see the cuts.
Tilly then offers a brief summary of the pros and cons.

Tilly: 'Ok, let's see if I've got this right. You like it that your cutting relieves stress and helps you to feel better. On the other hand, your main concerns are about how it upsets your Mum and what other people think about you. Is that right?'

Abby: 'Yeah.'

Tilly: 'So, having looked at both sides, where does that leave you now, Abby – what do you want your next move to be?'

COMMENT

In the case study above, the ownership of the next move rests with the young person. Tilly will listen for any change talk and self-motivating statements from Abby. When appropriate, she will offer information if she hears that Abby is at the point of readiness for change. The other skill that is evident in the conversation is that of reflective listening. Simply reflecting back the words of the young person will help to clarify meaning and encourage further exploration. When the young person begins to make change talk statements, reflecting these back can help to strengthen resolve, but the counsellor must be careful not to fall into the trap of advocating for what they feel is a necessary change. It is important to continue to reflect the client's perspective when resistance re-emerges in such situations.

ACTIVITY 7.1

• How would you respond in the follow situation?

Young person: 'My Mum is way too strict and I hate it, but I guess that's 'cause she worries about me.'

Counsellor: 'She cares about you enough to have rules about what you should do.'

Young person (sounding angry): 'Yeah, but the rules are ridiculous and it's not fair!'

COMMENT

To restore the balance the counsellor can offer a double-sided reflection to capture both sides of the conflict. The aim is for the young person to voice what needs to change and for them to work towards the direction of change. So the counsellor might respond with, 'You wish perhaps that she cared a bit less at times, because she goes over the top in trying to protect you.' Hopefully, the young person would then feel understood and reply with something along the lines of, 'Yeah, right. I mean I know she cares, but I just want her to trust me more and give me a bit more freedom.' When change talk starts occurring it needs to be affirmed, so that the young person can build self-efficacy. Simple feedback comments like, 'I can see how that is important for you' or 'That sounds like a good idea' can help in this regard.

4. Support self-efficacy

Self-efficacy refers to a person's belief in their ability to undertake and achieve success with a specific task or action in order to accomplish change (Bandura, 1977). A young person who perceives that there is an issue to work on, and acknowledges that they would like to change their behaviour, will not make that change if they feel it is beyond their capacity. For change to occur, both the counsellor and the young person must believe that the envisaged change is possible – they must be confident that barriers can be met and surmounted. In line with other approaches in this book, action steps and the resources to work towards those goals need to be motivational. This does not mean that the counsellor is inactive at this point; their role is to assist the young person to enhance their confidence to act for themselves.

OTHER TECHNIQUES

There are a number of other techniques within motivational interview that would need to be explored further by the counsellor wishing to use this approach. As indicated earlier, with change comes resistance and it is important to acknowledge that resistance arises in a dynamic relationship between the young person and the systems they are placed within, including the relationship with the practitioner. This can be due to a conflict around goals and aspiration, where the young person feels powerless to assert their views. In the counselling relationship it can result from a mismatch between the counsellor and the young person's view about readiness for change. Resistance can be identified when the young person argues, interrupts, negates that there is an issue and refuses to cooperate or simply ignores the counsellor. The point of listing these behaviours is not to seek ways of blaming the individual, but to identify what is going wrong in the counselling relationship that is hindering the young person's motivation towards change. The reflective listening skills discussed in an earlier chapter are useful when working with resistance, alongside the following.

- Shifting the focus away from stumbling blocks – go round them.
- Reframing by offering new meaning, while acknowledging the validity of the young person's observations.
- Agreeing with a twist, which involves an initial agreement followed by a slight change of direction to encourage a reframing of the issue.
- Emphasising personal choice and control to maintain freedom of choice.

- Coming alongside – sometimes referred to as 'reverse psychology' and the 'therapeutic paradox' – this is not to 'give up' on the problem, but places the responsibility for not changing back with the client.

That last point needs further explanation, and Miller and Rollnick have devoted much attention to this (2002, p107). This technique can be misinterpreted as the counsellor employing a clever trick – that is not the intention. The term 'coming alongside' is indicative of the principle of working with the client's ambivalence, looking to evoke change talk in the dialogue. It can be useful to defuse the arguments in defence of not changing. The aim is for the response from the counsellor to promote a decrease in resistance and a reverse movement from the young person towards engaging with the notion of change. Space here prevents a detailed discussion, but hopefully an example will aid understanding. Below is part of a conversation about making future choices in education.

Case study 7.3   Diagnosing resistance to change

Young person: 'Those courses are rubbish.'
Counsellor: 'What concerns do you have about them?'
Young person: 'They're just not gonna work for me.'
Counsellor (in a neutral voice): 'OK, I hear what you're saying. It's quite possible that after trying one you'll still be where you are now and things will not have improved, and so it may be better not to try any of them.'
(Pause)
Young person: 'Well, I dunno, if there's nothing else . . . maybe if I looked at them again there could be some new ones.'

COMMENT

Diagnosing resistance to change can be aided by the use of the 'wheel of change' to identify where the young person is in the change process. This is also referred to as the 'transtheoretical model of intentional human behavior change' (TTM) and can be explored further through the work of DiClemente and Velasquez (2002), among others.

THE WHEEL OF CHANGE

As can be seen in Figure 7.1, including pre-contemplation, there are six stages in the motivational interviewing diagnostic tool. Drawing on Rollnick and Miller (1995), these can be described as follows.

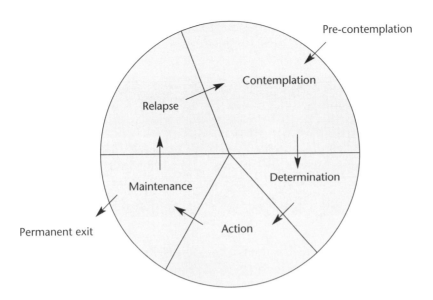

Figure 7.1: The wheel of change (Prochaska and DiClemente, 1982)

- **Pre-contemplation**. At this stage the young person has no intention of changing their behaviour, and may be unaware of the nature of the problem facing them. The behaviour demonstrated would be, 'I'm OK. Problem – what problem?'
- **Contemplation**. The young person is aware at this stage that the problem exists, but they are not yet committed to change, and may feel undecided, or may oscillate between desiring change and acceptance of the current situation. The behaviour demonstrated is ambivalent, 'I'm not sure, I don't know'.
- **Determination**. The young person has now made the decision to change and is motivated to move forward, but will need a clear goal, plan of action and support to make change happen. The behaviour is demonstrated by statements such us, 'I've decided, I know what I want to do'.
- **Action**. The young person is putting the decision into practice, supported by the counsellor. Together action is agreed, reviewed and redesigned. This may take some time, and there is a risk of relapse. The behaviour demonstrated is, 'I know what, and I think I know how, and I'm now taking my next steps'.
- **Maintenance**. By taking action the young person consolidates the change made to secure the new behaviour and works to avoid relapse. The counsellor works to enable the young person, withdrawing their support gradually as the young person becomes more confident. The behaviour demonstrated is, 'I can do this and I am getting there'.
- **Relapse**. The young person may, at any stage, fall back into the old behaviour. Change is not viewed as always linear in this model and it is recognised that a relapse is normal. The counsellor's role is to ensure

that this is seen as normal and expected behaviour, while supporting the young person to continue the process.

ACTIVITY 7.2

- Think about a young person you have worked with recently where the work appeared to be stuck. Use the wheel of change to evaluate what stage they were at and consider whether your interventions were helpful or not. Applying your reading from this chapter, what could you do differently?

Using the wheel of change can enable the counsellor to diagnose where a young person is in terms of the process of change. It helps to identify the young person's readiness for change and is useful for assessing appropriate support for the young person at each stage. Clearly, the early stages should not be rushed, as rushing a young person will make failure more likely if they are not ready to move forward. In summary, the particular strengths of utilising the wheel of change when working with young people are that it:

- offers an insight into where the young person may be in terms of their willingness and ability to change;
- provides a tool for analysis of where the young person may be 'stuck' in the process of change;
- recognises that 'relapse' is not viewed as failure, but as a temporary, though expected, setback to progress;
- helps the counsellor to question if their actions are congruent with the young person's position in terms of the change process, and thus
- avoids inappropriate interventions.

CHAPTER SUMMARY

This chapter has introduced the reader to the motivational interviewing approach which is envisaged as an effective method of communication for counselling work with young people. It has outlined the values that underpin the approach and discussed its general principles. In addition, the wheel of change has been suggested as a useful diagnostic tool for exploring 'stuckness' in terms of the young person's commitment to change. In turn, this can be used as a reflective tool for the counsellor to consider the balance between the actions they expect the young person to be taking, and what, in their own thinking and actions, may be hampering that movement.

Motivational interviewing is not a 'quick fix' solution or merely a bunch of techniques to be applied. It is underpinned by extensive research across a number of professional fields. Miller and Rollnick continue to revise the approach and welcome adaptations beyond the addiction field where it originated.

SUGGESTED FURTHER READING

Miller, WR and Rollnick, R (2002) *Motivational Interviewing: Preparing People for Change*, 2nd edition. New York: The Guilford Press.

The key text, full of case studies and examples of application in a range of settings. Aside from Miller and Rollnick's major contribution there are a number of chapters in the book from writers who have applied the approach within a range of settings.

In the spirit of openness and accessibility described above, there is a wealth of material on motivational interviewing on the web – putting the term into a search engine will result in access to original materials.

CHAPTER 8

Working with solution-focused approaches for counselling young people

by Hazel Reid

CORE KNOWLEDGE

By the end of this chapter you will have the opportunity to:

- read about the foundations of solution-focused counselling;
- note the factors to be considered before using the approach;
- evaluate how solution-focused counselling could be used in your own work;
- identify the advantages of using the approach with young people.

INTRODUCTION

Solution-focused counselling does what it says on the tin. In other words, it focuses on solutions rather than problems. The counsellor adopting this approach uses a number of strategies and skills that take a forward-looking stance, where 'problems' are redefined as part of moving towards a solution. This chapter explains solution-focused counselling and gives examples of the skills and 'future-orientated' questions that can be used in practice. Many of the solution-focused strategies can be integrated into other models and approaches. But first it is important, as always, to gain an overview of the approach and understand the conceptual foundations of solution-focused counselling.

In assisting young people to find ways of managing the issue that brings them to counselling, counsellors working from this approach do not spend time exploring or analysing problems in detail. Solution-focused counselling pays attention to finding solutions based on what is working already, in order to look for clues about what will work in the future. A solution-focused approach assumes that change is inevitable as, because the young person is seeking or has been referred for counselling, change is viewed as happening currently. The counsellor's role is to help the young person build on their strengths. The aim is to develop motivation through enhancing the young person's sense of what is possible. This is achieved by working alongside the client to avoid taking an expert position, rather than working as the 'helper' who holds the answers to the problem.

As in other approaches described in this book, solution-focused counselling uses the foundational skills of rapport building and listening to the young person's story. While the title is appealing – perhaps suggesting a 'quick fix' for counselling young people – the approach stresses the need to take time, to search for the detail so that action taken will be purposeful, but also meaningful to the young person. Terms in common parlance such as 'solution focused', 'outcome focused' and 'building on what works', have an allure that can be engaging, but premature action can be at best pointless, and at worst, damaging. As with all approaches discussed in this book, it is fundamental that the young person is listened to and that their view is acknowledged and respected. That said, although the work will not dwell on 'problem-saturated' stories (see Chapter 9), the counsellor must avoid moving too quickly to discussions about change. However, providing a safe space for dreaming and focusing on a possible future can encourage a spirit of hopefulness; clearly, the relationship and sense of timing is the means to make this happen. Creating and maintaining the therapeutic relationship takes time and, of course, is central in ensuring that the young person can engage effectively with any counselling process (Green, 2010).

So, to repeat the point, the approach is outcome-focused in that it explores solutions rather than problems and involves the counsellor focusing on what the young person has already achieved. This involves 'positive talk' where problems are redefined as part of moving towards a solution, rather than staying with a discussion of issues that have to be understood. Like narrative counselling, this shifts from viewing the person as the problem, but sees the problem as simply something the person wishes to be without (de Shazer, 1988). Put another way, this entails moving away from understanding why something is the way it is, towards what solutions would look like, and how those solutions or goals can be reached. The starting point in building rapport within the therapeutic relationship is to ensure that the young person's concerns are acknowledged. Once these are shared, the counsellor and young person can cultivate ways of reframing the problem to help make change possible.

REFLECTION POINT

- Before continuing, try to summarise your understanding so far by completing the following sentence – 'I think the main features of solution-focused counselling could be described as . . .'

FOUNDATIONAL CONCEPTS OF SOLUTION-FOCUSED COUNSELLING

The founding members of the Brief Family Therapy Team in Milwaukee, Wisconsin, USA were led by Steve de Shazer (de Shazer et al., 1986). What is meant by 'brief' therapy is discussed below, but first, this section outlines the future focus of the approach. Rather than concentrate on the history of the problem, the team noted that conversations with clients which focused on preferred futures were equally effective in terms of leading to change. Clients appeared keen to describe what a future could be like. The solutions for making change happen were not always linked directly to the problem, but the solutions were closely connected to the goals of the client, once these were discovered through the forward-thinking process. Once solutions were articulated and the focus of the conversation shifted to discussing these, the problem was regarded differently and often its significance was reduced (O'Connell, 2001). The strategies that the team developed, based on future-orientated questions, were seen as 'keys' to unlocking the solutions to the presenting issue. Choosing to move away from focusing on the problem, the conversations paid attention to non-problematic behaviour and to personal competences and strengths (O'Connell, 2001).

Focusing on the future does not mean ignoring the past: our past shapes who we are, but does not determine who we might become. O'Connell explains:

> *Young people, in particular, are more willing to invest time in finding out what they could become than in what has gone before. Knowing how to get the life you want is often more attractive than working out how you got the one you have.*

> (2001, p6)

A focus on past events – what has gone before – might be the lay person's view of psychotherapy. Dryden and Feltham (1992) do not make a distinction between counselling and psychotherapy in terms of what both try to achieve, that is, to alleviate distress and find solutions to problems in order to assist people to lead lives that are more satisfying. They do not see counselling as 'brief' or, in other words, superficial, when compared to long-term psychotherapy. The length of 'treatment' is, they note, a matter of contention and, contrary to many assumptions, it is psychoanalytical practitioners who have been in the vanguard of calls to condense therapy (Flegenheimer, 1982). This has led, Dryden and Feltham claim, to the emergence of cognitive-behavioural and other related approaches. When using the term 'brief', this can mean from one to up to twenty sessions and may be weekly or over a longer time period – in other words, there is no standard pattern for the work, although within the public services sector a pattern of six to eight sessions is common. Focusing on the main concerns that bring a person to counselling, within a context that pays attention to costs and time, has been argued to shorten therapy and lead to change more efficiently (Malan, 1975;

Balint et al., 1972). Writing about a solution-focused approach for school counsellors, Sklare (2005) notes that with over 500 students in a case load, there is little time for long-term counselling. What is needed, he states, is a focused approach that can be implemented across a range of issues.

Space limits the discussion on the differences between counselling and longer-term therapy and, to avoid any confusion, the term Solution Focused Brief Therapy (SFBT) will not be used in this chapter: the term solution-focused counselling will be used. That said, there is some consensus within the literature with regard to the main characteristics of planned brief therapy, summarised by Barrett-Kruse as:

- *the view that self and others are essentially able;*
- *the acceptance of the client's definition of the problem;*
- *the formation of the therapeutic alliance;*
- *the crediting of success to the client;*
- *the therapist learning from the client;*
- *the avoidance of a power struggle with the client;*
- *the objectification rather than the personalisation of the client's behaviour.*

(1994, pp109–15)

REFLECTION POINT

- Many of the above characteristics could be applied to other approaches encountered so far in this book, but what about the last point – what does it mean to you, what are the implications of personalising the client's behaviour? If you are not sure, look back at Chapter 4 on multiculturalism for an explanation.

Solution-focused counselling needs to be distinguished from time-limited therapy: the latter stipulates a specific and therefore limited number of sessions available. In solution-focused counselling:

> brief means an ethical commitment to work economically, simply and efficiently with minimal intrusion into the client's life. For brief counselling to be effective, the counsellor needs to believe that it is qualitatively different from long-term work, not inferior to it but different.
>
> (O'Connell, 2001, p4)

Bill O'Connell is closely associated with solution-focused counselling and therapy (2005). He points out that there are many different strands within the solution-focused school of practice but, despite variations, what binds them is that they stand 'in opposition to therapies influenced by the medical model or to ones which see the therapist as an expert' (2001, p1). O'Connell welcomes approaches in counselling that can encompass ideas and techniques from a broad range. A solution-focused approach does not mean that for every problem there is only one solution. Solutions will vary and be as different as individual clients, their issues, the meaning that those issues have for them, and all set within their particular context. Alongside drawing on knowledge of a range of approaches, the counsellor will work with the young person to discover and respect the young person's own way of creating meaningful solutions. This will include cultural solutions that may be outside of the counsellor's experience. But, searching for solutions does not mean rushing to action. A foundational concept in solution-focused counselling is that no matter how difficult or stressful the situation may be, the young person will have resources to draw upon, times when things were better, when they were effective, but (and it is a significant but) these resources have become lost or hidden in the problem. The work will aim to focus on what the young person can do with support, not what the counsellor can suggest in order to 'help' and solve the problem. So rather than exploring the past or the causes of underlying issues, the counselling conversation is future-orientated.

ACTIVITY 8.1

At this point, it should be clear that there is a significant difference between an approach that explores the problem or issue and one that focuses on solutions. The following table distinguishes between the two.

- Look at Table 8.1 and, reflecting, on your reading so far, fill in the blanks.

Problem-focused approach	Solution-focused approach
From problem	To solution
Past	
Causes	Multiple description
	How questions
What happened?	What do you want?
Insight/cure/growth	
Deep	Surface
	Collaborative approach
What is wrong?	
Client learns from counsellor	Counsellor learns from client
Long and painful	
	Solutions fit the person
Expert language	
Resistance	Cooperation

Table 8.1. Characteristics of problem-focused and solution-focused counselling approaches. Adapted from O'Connell (2001, p6)

Of course, the above presents a dichotomous (either/or) positioning in terms of the focus of the conversation within the counselling approach. However, in solution-focused work there will be time spent exploring the problem and the counsellor will, of course, spend time listening to the client in order to acknowledge and validate what is meaningful and important for them – the client. If this were not done, the therapeutic relationship would not be built successfully. Nevertheless, the intention is to move to future-orientated and strategy talk to build solutions according to the client's priorities, which in turn can help to reframe the problem. Returning to the activity above, you may have used different expressions to fill in the gaps, but hopefully these will have a similar meaning to those found in O'Connell's table (see the end of the chapter for the missing words).

THE PROCESS

Before moving on, it is important to spend a little time thinking about structure or process. At the beginning of this book, and in each chapter, it has been emphasised that within the space available what can be offered is an introduction only. At the end of this chapter further reading is, once again, suggested in order to broaden and deepen your understanding of solution-focused work within counselling. It may be worth pointing out that this is not a model with rigid steps to be followed, for instance first one technique followed by another: fitting the young person into a list of techniques. There is a process, a structure, but this should be used flexibly. In Chapter 2 a model for structuring counselling work with young people was offered, based on the work of Egan (2007). Solution-focused counselling would fit into this model, but there would be some differences in terms of focus within each stage across the whole counselling process. Readers should investigate this further through the literature (for example, O'Connell, 2001; 2005), as a summary here will be reductive. However, moving straight to techniques without a brief summary is unlikely to be helpful, so the beginning stage (the first session) would focus on:

- contracting and identifying what the client wishes to pay attention to in order to establish their priorities;
- problem-free talk to build rapport and initiate a preliminary look for strengths and resources;
- explanation and exploration of the theme of change;
- goal setting for the work.

The middle stage (the second and subsequent sessions) would focus on:

- continuing to identify change and seek for 'news' of what is different;
- amplifying any changes made by focusing on the effects of the change;

- reinforcing the change that is leading to the elicited goals;
- identifying other changes, using respectful curiosity.

The ending stage should be discussed at the beginning as part of contracting. In other words, it is likely that there are a defined number of sessions in 'brief' counselling. Preparation for ending the relationship is vital in order to avoid dependency. If the number of sessions is not predetermined, then endings should take place as soon as the client is confident to work on the changes on their own. Strategies for evaluating that this point has been reached could include scaling – one of the techniques associated with solution-focused counselling (more on this later in the chapter).

> ### REFLECTION POINT
>
> - Solution-focused counselling is seen as particularly useful for working with young people in schools. Before looking at the techniques, note down what you view as the factors or constraints that need to be considered before using the approach with young people in schools. It may help to think about the context, the location of the counselling room, the age range of the clients or other aspects that may have an impact on counselling.
> - Would there be presenting issues where you feel solution-focused counselling would not be the appropriate approach?

COMMENT

What you noted in the above will depend on your knowledge of counselling in a school or educational environment, neither of which may be the context for your practice. Nonetheless, such aspects are probably not unique to schools and are worth consideration. Lines (2006), working with young people in the age range from 11 to 18 in schools, notes that there are limitations using any counselling approach within educational contexts. For a start, the counsellor must consider what is achievable within a setting where the provision of a quiet space, privacy and confidentiality can be compromised by both the physical structures and the rules of the school. The power relations within a school can also disable a young person seeking or 'sent' for counselling. In addition to the techniques that are suitable within the school and wider cultural community, counsellors have to consider the aims of counselling; the resources available; how to plan and sustain counselling programmes; the counselling styles and methods that various students will be comfortable with; the appropriateness of particular approaches in terms of the issues to be worked with. Compromises may have to be made within an approach, which must remain ethical. For Lines, working within the constraints of a school setting, 'brief' counselling that draws on solution-focused, alongside other approaches, can be effective, even when time is limited and a confidential setting is hard to preserve.

TECHNIQUES WITHIN SOLUTION-FOCUSED COUNSELLING

Moving on, what follows are explanations of some of the core techniques that are found within solution-focused work – this is not an exhaustive account, but should provide enough insight to whet the appetite to find out more.

Seeking exceptions to the problem

For some young people there will be many problems and issues to deal with and it can be difficult to know where to start. Solution-focused counselling would stress that urgent issues need to be attended to first, but it is the young person who decides the priority, not the counsellor. Exception seeking asks the young person to describe a time when the issue to be worked on was less of a problem or not evident. The assumption here is that there will always be times when the problem is absent, or less of a problem, or not the same. Identifying these times can help the young person and the counsellor to explore how those conditions can be repeated. When under stress and overwhelmed by current, and often troubling events, we can all lose a sense of perspective; thus identifying exceptions may help the young person to feel that change is possible, despite the current circumstances.

Exception seeking can involve 'micro talk' where the counsellor searches for the detail that is concealed in what the young person is saying. Here are some possible questions.

- What happened next?
- And then what happened?
- What were you thinking?
- What else was happening at the time?
- Who else was around?
- How did that feel?

The aim is to stay with the story about the time when the problem was absent, or less of a problem, or not the same. Many young people will find this difficult and will be suspicious if they think this is some kind of 'mind game', which they then find uncomfortable. As with any approach, it is both helpful and congruent to explain what it is you are trying to do and why, for instance, 'I'd like us to explore the times when the issue was not so significant in your life. Will it be OK to ask you some detailed questions, so that we can understand what was going on and use what we find to think about what might be helpful now?'

The counsellor will then need to be attentive to any exceptions in the young person's responses, for example a reply that is not completely negative can lead to the discovery of an exception. For instance, the word 'sometimes' suggests an opening to explore the 'other times'. 'Maybe', suggests there could be something more to explore, although the counsellor should be careful not to breach the young person's defences.

Scaling

Expecting a young person to talk coherently about a problem and their feelings in relation to it can be asking too much, particularly when there are a number of issues, or when they are feeling confused or anxious. The technique of scaling can help to express thoughts and feelings about issues or problems through the use of numbers. The scale ranges from 0 to 10, with 0 representing the worst case and 10 representing a time when the problem may no longer exist. It can help to engage the young person in the evaluation of their current situation and their views about possible future goals. If a young person describes their current position on the scale as, say, three, together the counsellor and young person can discuss what needs to happen to raise this to a higher score – but not too high; the increase must be reasonable.

Case study 8.1   Scaling in practice

Sam (the counsellor): 'Tell me, Jazmin, how you are feeling today on a scale from 0 to 10, where 0 is the worst it has ever been and 10 would be a time when the problem had disappeared.'

Jazmin: 'About a three, I suppose.'

Sam: 'OK, so that we can work on this together – what would you say needs to happen for you to score this at, say, a 3½ or 4 on the scale?'

It is also important to recognise that the problem's influence will vary; thus, scaling is a technique that can be used regularly. As mentioned earlier, scaling can also be used in the ending stage of the process to evaluate the change that has been achieved.

Building on strengths

Solution-focused counselling aims to build on the young person's strengths. The strengths and skills identified then become resources that can be used to find solutions to the current issue. This may be drawing on past experience, but it also takes account of present competences that are helpful in relation to the future that the young person begins to envisage. It can highlight what has been tried and found to be helpful. It can also identify what has been tried and found to be unhelpful. This is likely to require persistence from the counsellor, particularly if working with a young person who does not believe they have strengths or is reluctant to engage with the process. But the aim is to move out of a conversation style that dwells on problems and negativity, to one that focuses on solutions.

O'Connell (2001) suggests that even when clients are stuck in 'problem talk' the counsellor can ask coping questions that hunt for the young person's hidden resources. To illustrate this, the following questions look for strengths, exceptions and include a scaling question.

- *How do you cope with all that is happening to you?*
- *What helps you when things are different?*
- *Has it got worse or is this the worst it has ever been?*
- *Are you stronger now than you were last month/year?*
- *Which was the least bad day last week?*
- *Which was the best day?*
- *How does coming here help?*
- *On a scale of 0–10, with 0 being as bad as it's ever been, where would you say you were today?*

(O'Connell, 2001, pp17–18)

And, of course, searching for the detail through 'micro talk' would draw on the questions suggested earlier, for example 'What happened next?' and so on. And, an easy 'probe' to remember, that helps to avoid a string of questions, is 'Tell me more about that'.

This kind of questioning, and use of the scaling technique, will help the counsellor make an assessment of the young person's current position and counselling needs without the imposition of externally produced tests, which can often lead to alienation. However, using this kind of questioning, particularly when it receives a 'Dunno' answer, or no answer and a shrug, needs practice. Resistance from the young person can produce feelings of irritation in the counsellor. A reflexive counsellor will regard a negative response as a form of communication, indicating that there is a disparity between what the young person needs and what they (the counsellor) are doing. A counsellor can use this as a sign that they should change their approach and do something different (O'Connell, 2001).

Asking questions about a possible future

Redefining the problem as part of moving towards a solution does not ignore the perceived constraints of a young person's situation and these constraints need to be explored. This is not the same as seeing the young person as somehow damaged, incompetent, lacking in resources and defined by the issues brought to counselling. The solution-focused process acknowledges the situation but explores it from the point of view of the young person who, because they are there, is seen as wanting to make a change. In this way the counsellor demonstrates their belief in the young person's ability to effect change. This belief is necessary before engaging in talk about a possible future and proposals for making change happen. The miracle question (see below) is a useful technique for assisting young people to look forward to the future. And, in looking at goals for the future, questions such as, 'How would you recognise that had happened?', and the follow up, 'What would that feel like?' are helpful to depict that possibility further. But first, the next section will examine the miracle question in some detail.

Using the miracle question

The miracle question is a central technique within the solution-focused approach. It can be used to assist young people to express their hopes, which may be buried by the issues they face, and it can help to identify the resources that can support them to work towards an identified goal. In addition, it can be applied for detecting past achievements that are related to the aspirations that are articulated, which, in turn, can help to devise strategies and appropriate action. As with any potentially 'surprising' intervention, it helps to introduce it by saying something like, 'I'm going to ask you a question now that may sound a little strange, but we may find this helpful in thinking about the future.'

So, the classic miracle question (de Shazer, 1988) can be adapted for working with young people in order to help them to think about a possible future. It goes something like this:

> *Imagine when you go to sleep one night a miracle happens and the problems that we've been talking about disappear. As you were asleep, you did not know that a miracle had happened. When you woke up what would be the first signs for you that a miracle had happened?*

This is a powerful technique and can create a turning point in the session and in the overall work with a young person, but there are cautions that need to be considered. The careful timing of the question is critical. Rapport within the therapeutic relationship between the counsellor and the young person must be well established, and this includes ensuring that the young person's story has been heard and understood in terms of its meaning for them. It moves from talk about the problem to exploration of the preferred future, where the problem is set aside for the moment. It can also help to bring some focus for a young person who feels 'weighed down' by the issues they face. It can be difficult for the young person to be specific about which problems to talk about in the opening stage, when the issues seem overwhelming. The risk here is that the counsellor can introduce a focusing intervention too soon in the relationship. However, an exploration of a 'miracle' future can help to disclose the nature of the barrier that is preventing the young person from thinking ahead.

Of course, the problem might be a matter that cannot be sorted out even in an imaginary situation. An inappropriately used technique will leave the young person feeling more immobilised and the counsellor feeling as if they have heightened the problem. For example, a young person who has lost a parent, or has a medical condition that is disabling them in some significant way, may respond with an answer that appears to increase the problem, rather than one that visualises a changed future. For instance, 'My mum would still be alive' as the miracle, would be cited in a problem that could not be overcome. If the counsellor is aware beforehand that the presenting issue derives from a traumatic event, such as bereavement, then solution-focused counselling would not be the approach to draw on. Staying within a person-centred approach, which provides a safe 'holding' space (Winnicott, 1965) to 'contain' (Bion, 1970) the young person's emotions, would be more appropriate, in contrast to an approach that is solution-focused. If not trained for bereavement counselling, the counsellor may decide to discuss with the young person a referral to a colleague who does have expertise in this area. If unsure how to proceed; the issue should be discussed within supervision. To summarise, it is essential that the miracle question is introduced thoughtfully and appropriately, and, using the word 'miracle' may not always be helpful.

Case study 8.2   Jamial

Jamial is 15 and was referred to Josh (the school counsellor) as his behaviour in school was described as withdrawn. Josh is told that previous to this current year, Jamial engaged well in most aspects of his school work. His tutor is very concerned, as Jamial's inconsistent attendance is now also becoming an issue and 'he seems to be on a downward spiral'. Josh has seen Jamial on two previous occasions and in the last session, Jamial trusted him enough to tell him he was 'bullied last year, a lot, on the way home from school'.

Since the family has moved to another area the bullying has ceased, but Jamial's self-esteem and confidence remains very low. Josh has spent time listening to how Jamial feels now about the bullying, and in the previous session they used the scaling technique. They repeated the technique in this third meeting, but the 'score' Jamial gives for his feelings about the bullying has not shifted. Once settled into this third meeting, Josh tries using a miracle question.

Josh: 'This question may sounds a bit odd, Jamial, but I'd like to try something to help us think ahead to a time when things may feel different to how they do

---

today. The bullying last year was a very bad experience and we won't forget that as we continue to work together. We cannot change what's happened, but I wonder what a future would look like where a change had occurred and the bullying does not feel as horrible as it does at the moment? How would you know that that change had taken place?'

Jamial: 'I wouldn't feel so crap all the time.'

Josh: 'You wouldn't feel so crap all the time, so what would be the signs that things were different?'

Jamial: 'The signs? I dunno, maybe I'd be enjoying stuff again.'

Josh: 'Yes that would be a sign – what stuff Jamial, anything in particular?'

Jamial (pause): 'I always liked sport in school, particularly football.'

Josh: 'What would that be like to be enjoying football again? Tell me more about what would be happening.'

Jamial: 'Well I was in the school team but got dropped because I missed sessions.'

Josh: 'So, let's assume you are back in the team, what would that be like?'

Jamial: 'Good, but I think I've blown it.'

Josh: 'Well, if you are OK to keep exploring this, Jamial, we'll think about how you can get back into the team later, if that's what you decide you want, but for now, can we stay with this a bit longer?'

Jamial: 'Yeah, OK.'

Josh: 'So, let's imagine you are back in the team, how would you be feeling?'

Jamial: 'A bit strange at first 'cause I've missed sessions, but I played well with me mates before.'

Josh: 'Ah, so you're good at football, then – is that what I'm hearing?'

COMMENT

The intention here is to help the young person to construct a more hopeful story where the problem does not define their life. Josh would develop the questioning to identify the strengths that Jamial can use (connected to being part of a team, performing well and being valued by others); in order to help define a future goal and work towards it (feeling less 'crap'/'enjoying stuff'/ feeling confident and getting back in the team). Josh would also be looking for exceptions to the problem: to identify the times and conditions when Jamial can act successfully to achieve the first steps towards the elicited goal.

A further use of this questioning technique for other situations, at the appropriate time, could be, 'If you woke up tomorrow and you could start the job of your dreams, what sorts of things would you be doing in that job?' The point is not to name an occupation and how to get there, but to keep the focus on the positive aspects of the dream. This can be refined to include, 'people you would be working with', 'places you would be doing the job' and so on. The same type of question can be used for those who want to enter further education, but have no idea of the type of course. If the prospect of work or education or training is too far beyond the current possibilities for a dream, then the question can be used about friendship groups, family or other close relationships or fundamental issues concerning health, somewhere to live and aspects of personal safety and well-being.

Assisting the young person to imagine and articulate the dream will require the skill of micro questioning to 'dig' for the detail. Useful questions, as above, can include: 'What would that be like?', 'What would you notice?', 'How would you be feeling at that point?', 'And then what would happen?' and the prompt 'Tell me more about . . .' At the same time the counsellor will be looking for the threads in the possible future that can be woven into the present, and vice versa. As with all questioning techniques within counselling, it is important that this does not turn into a series of questions that alienate the young person; this can happen if they feel they are being 'tested' in some way. The intention is to identify exceptions and resources that can be used to agree appropriate action steps towards articulating 'the miracle', not to interrogate the young person.

> *Used well, and even creatively, the hypothetical or miracle question encourages the young person to view themselves as having some agency, in other words it opens up the possibility of a different, and potentially empowering, view of self.*
>
> (Reid, 2008, p475)

It is essential, however, that both the young person and the counsellor work together to create achievable goals, to take the dream beyond the sheltered space of the counselling room. The miracle question, without that ongoing support, will not be liberating unless both parties work collaboratively to turn a view of self that is negative, into one that is positive. Asking, 'So what are you going to do to make the miracle happen?' is not supportive and is likely to feel confrontational, leading to defensiveness. It is, in short, asking too much of a vulnerable young person. To enable a young person to envisage their world and their place within it differently, counsellors need patience, and young people need support and time.

Taking one small step at a time

Patience means agreeing and setting small goals that can lead to a sense of achievement when these are met. For many young people who may not view themselves as successful, this can be a very positive process in building confidence and self-esteem. The view of self can change from 'I'm a failure' (along with all the possible linked behaviour) to 'I'm an achiever'.

Getting the young person to do something different

The solution-focused approach recognises that when people are stuck in their problems they often repeat behaviour and action that is known to them, even when the outcome highlights the futility of their past behaviour. In other words, when stuck, continuing to do the same thing (which is 'safe' because it is known) leads to the same result; doing something different (which is unknown) is scary and so avoided. A solution-focused approach would not work to analyse why the behaviour arose, but would look for acceptable alternatives to try out in order to identify helpful action that promotes change. Talking about the behaviour may help, as being listened to has potency, but doing something different, it is argued, leads to change. In this way solutions are tried that fit the young person, rather than proposing 'answers' to the problem (Winslade and Monk, 2007).

Doing something different recognises that if something does not work (past, present or future), then it is sensible to stop doing it and do something else. But it is the young person, supported by the counsellor, who considers the advantages of stopping the current behaviour and trying something new. It is therefore essential to evaluate the results of the new behaviour and decide together what was valuable and how it helped, in relation to the agreed goals.

Complimenting the young person on what they are doing right

Attending or being 'sent' for counselling runs the risk of labelling young people in a variety of negative ways (for example, school phobic, drug user, self-harmer, bully, depressive, and so on). Compliments are 'positive strokes' and enhance the young person's view of self, but young people become skilful at identifying a false compliment. Used with congruence, compliments encourage equality in a relationship where both the counsellor and young person are engaged in a learning process. Compliments can be used in any of the strategies outlined above in order to reward a young person for an action taken in the past, present, or an action they are thinking about trying in the future.

Many of the techniques above are appealing as they are relatively easy to describe and the theory behind them can be demonstrated in practice (Myers, 2007), but like any other approach described in this book, they will not work all the time with all young people. Thus, if something does not work, from the solution-focused perspective, the counsellor would stop doing it; and if something does work, they would keep on doing it. This flexibility is imperative for both the counsellor in their practice and for the young person in their thinking about their current situation and their future action. And, of course, if agreed action towards achievable goals does not prove useful, then the counsellor should acknowledge that and share responsibility for this, within a 'non-blaming' and collaborative approach.

ACTIVITY 8.2

- Think of a young person you have worked with where the work was difficult or appeared to get stuck. Would a solution-focused approach, using any of these techniques, have made a difference? How – in what way?
- Write down, or discuss with a colleague, what the practice difficulty was and how the approach and techniques might help in a similar situation.

If it isn't broken, don't fix it!

The solution-focused approach avoids seeing the individual as defined by their problem, but beyond this, the approach focuses on strengths and the things that the client does well. Psychology, psychotherapy and counselling can all exacerbate a problem if unhappiness, as part of the normal human condition and passage through life, is pathologised (Parker, 2007). The question should always be asked – for whom is this particular issue a problem? If a person has the reserves, the strengths, the support to manage their unhappiness, they may not require an intervention by a professional. Thus, the principle of 'If it isn't broken, don't fix it', reminds counsellors to tread carefully and not to assume they have the right to intervene in any aspect of a young person's life.

CHAPTER SUMMARY

The intention of this chapter was not to suggest that solution-focused counselling and its adaptations are in any way superior to any of the other approaches outlined in this book. Although separate approaches are presented in this book, there are many common factors, which are perhaps more significant than the supposed differences. It is also important to say that there will be times when long-term psychotherapeutic work will be required and an appropriate referral for a young person will be necessary. This would be the case whatever counselling method is used, but requires repeating here in a chapter that has introduced a 'brief' approach. What the chapter has offered is an introduction to the approach and a description of solution-focused techniques. As presented in this chapter and drawing on the work of O'Connell (2001), the contribution that a solution-focused model can offer to counselling young people, can be summed up as follows:

- avoids negative assumptions about a young person;
- does not have to start with the history of the problem;
- balances exploration of the problem with strategies for constructing solutions;

- nurtures hope and optimism;
- avoids problem-saturated stories;
- draws on the young person's creativity to find solutions;
- helps to identify specific goals and actions;
- offers short-term rewards in terms of success;
- foregrounds the unique resourcefulness of a young person;
- outlines techniques that can be integrated into other approaches;
- reduces the danger of dependency;
- is accessible and appeals to young people.

Before leaving this discussion on solution-focused work, a final word of warning is perhaps necessary. Although a forward-looking approach can get a young person moving to action relatively quickly, benefits gained will not be sustained if the wider context of the young person's life is not given due consideration. An outcome-focused approach may fit nicely into a funding agenda which seeks ready-made solutions, but should not be viewed as an economical way of 'fixing' young people quickly. In addition, some young people, for a variety of reasons, may not engage with solution-focused counselling. When that happens, counsellors adopting an integrated approach should be flexible enough to change course and try something else.

SUGGESTED FURTHER READING

Lines, D (2006) *Brief Counselling in Schools: Working with Young People from 11 to 18*, 2nd edition. London: Sage.

This book is particularly useful for counsellors working in educational contexts with young people, as it recognises the constraints for practice. It is based on a method of brief integrative counselling that has wide application. It provides case study examples and this second edition includes working with anger, violence and aggression in schools.

O'Connell, B (2001) *Solution-Focused Stress Counselling*. London: Continuum.

O'Connell, B (2005) *Solution-Focused Therapy*, 2nd edition. London: Sage.

O'Connell is a leading practitioner and writer in the field of brief and solution-focused counselling, and both texts are highly recommended. Accessible and full of examples and case studies, they are comprehensive texts that will provide in-depth understanding for solution-focused counselling and therapeutic work.

Winslade, J and Monk, G (2007) *Narrative Counseling in Schools: Powerful and Brief*, 2nd edition, Thousand Oaks, California: Corwin Press.

Another accessible book that is particularly useful for working with young people. It provides outstanding examples and case studies. It is also mentioned in the chapter on narrative counselling as it skilfully combines narrative and brief counselling.

And the missing words in Activity 8.1 are, in order of appearance in the table: Future; Why questions; Change; Counsellor led; What is right?; Treatment fits the problem; Utilises a client's frame and language.

CHAPTER 9

Engaging young people through the use of a narrative approach to counselling

by Hazel Reid

CORE KNOWLEDGE

By the end of this chapter you will have the opportunity to:

- explore the ideas that underpin narrative counselling;
- consider the key concepts of the approach;
- identify practices that could be incorporated into counselling work with young people;
- reflect on how narrative thinking can be applied to your own practice.

INTRODUCTION

All therapies use counselling skills and, it could be said, all therapies rely on narratives. The word narrate is from the Latin *narrare*, 'to tell', and is derivative in other Indo-European languages, linked to the Latin words *gnarus* and *cognoscere*, broadly meaning 'to know'. Until we know where the person is positioned currently in their life story we cannot make an assessment to consider the type of intervention that is likely to prove useful. Using the word 'assessment', however, does not imply the use of a scientific test that allows us to measure the counselling needs of a young person in order to make objective decisions. Life as lived is subjective. Counsellors need to listen to the stories people tell them, but within the narrative approach this is a different kind of listening. It is not merely a listening for clues about what to do next, but a profound listening in order to discover how the young person structures their view of themselves via the stories they tell. The counsellor should search for other voices present in the stories told, as a subjective life is experienced in a context, with others. Engaging young people in counselling can be difficult if the presenting problem limits their ability to articulate their current story; the deeper listening to stories involved in the narrative approach aims to address this by encouraging a more developed description – a richer story.

This chapter discusses the thinking that underpins the narrative approach and outlines some of the key concepts and activities that can be explored further. As with other chapters in the book, what is included here is an introduction only. As stated in previous chapters, young people who seek or are referred to a counsellor will have different and possibly multiple issues to work through. The youth counsellor will need a range of strategies to work collaboratively with a person in order to engage them in the process. The arguments for and against integration will not be repeated here, but we need to be mindful that what follows should be adapted to the needs of particular young people. Thus, ideas from any approach must be evaluated for their usefulness for counselling work in different economic and social contexts.

Narrative counselling, like other constructivist approaches, pays attention to individual meaning by placing it, respectfully, in the foreground rather than in the background of other 'more important' issues (constructivism was discussed previously in Chapter 8). In other words, before exploring solutions to problems, the focus remains on the meaning the young person places on their situation. That said, each development of counselling practice can be thought of as a sedimentary layer built on earlier foundations of theory. The development of narrative therapy is not therefore a rejection of other models, and the idea that there could be one approach that would fit all young people is counter to a stance that advocates flexibility. Within the literature, evidence is cited for the effective use of narrative approaches when working with young people (Besley, 2002; Winslade and Monk, 2007). However, McLeod notes (1997) that research studies have focused on the practice of using narrative approaches rather than on evaluating the outcomes. Effectiveness, though, can be demonstrated through the use of case studies (for example, Payne, 2006) and this chapter takes a similar approach.

NARRATIVE THINKING

Issues related to power are at the heart of the narrative approach to counselling. Counsellors who work from this approach are concerned with taking an ethical and moral position in terms of how information is gathered about a young person, and how a counselling space can be developed that is collaborative and 'agentic'. In other words, the counsellor recognises that therapy can be part of the problem if the power relations within which a young person accesses counselling are not recognised. Young people operate within a socio-economic, cultural and historical context, and the problems they bring to counselling cannot be separated from the power-based relations that exist in their communities and the wider society. Payne states:

> *Narrative therapists recognise that persons sometimes ascribe the distressing and unjust results of these social factors to themselves, as personal*

failures, shortcomings or faults, and that they are often implicitly encouraged to do so by those who hold positions of power.

(2006, p12)

A reflexive counsellor will attempt to counter this potential in their own approach by continuous critical examination of the power relations in their practice.

ACTIVITY 9.1

- In your work setting, what are the wider power relations that can have an impact on the relationships that you have with young people in the counselling room? Think about aspects such as the goals of the organisation; the language used about young people and their problems; the funding for the activity; the time you have available; the physical space you counsel in; any outcomes or targets that you are expected to reach; your gender, age, ethnicity; your 'usual' counselling approach; your status as a professional counsellor.
- Now do the same from the perspective of a young person attending for counselling (it may help to think of a particular young person with whom you are working). How would their perspective on these aspects differ?

Before moving on, some 'unpacking' of the terms 'reflective' and 'reflexive' may be useful. Like so many terms in the social sciences, and the therapeutic and research literature, that unpacking is not straightforward and the concept is contested (Speedy, 2008). So, what follows attempts some illumination but recognises that in doing so, many arguments are left packed rather than unpacked. A reflective practitioner is someone who is able to reach potential solutions through analysing experience and prior knowledge – based on theory and practice – in order to inform current and future practice. This type of reflection does occur during a counselling session, but more often it happens later – in the car on the way home or in supervision. Reflexivity is a deeper process by which we are aware of our own responses to what is happening within a particular context (a counselling interaction) and our reactions to people, events and the dialogue taking place. A reflexive understanding will include an awareness of the personal, social and cultural context, and how it influences the process of counselling. Such a reflexive awareness leads to a greater understanding of how we co-construct knowledge about the world and ways of 'being' in it.

Etherington (2004, p29) suggests that this reflexivity in counselling practice, *involves operating on at least two levels*: first, inner reflection, which includes an ability to be aware of the impact of our behaviour on the counselling process and, second, a conscious awareness of our thoughts, feelings and imaginings within our minds and bodies. Etherington describes this as the need *to know the inner story that we tell ourselves as we listen to our clients' stories* (2004, p29). This is a deeper metacognitive process – thinking about thinking – that can lead to changes in the way we communicate with the young person and ourselves. It can enhance the relationship and lead to more collaborative work, acknowledging and fostering the individual's agency to effect change that is meaningful for them (Reid and Bassot, 2011). For the counsellor, it assists them to be fully conscious of and act upon the subjective influences that have an impact on their practice.

Aside from reflective processes, another way of addressing the imbalance of power is to make a practice of asking young people if what you are doing is acceptable and useful to them. This can be achieved by using open questions such as 'tell me, in what way is it useful?', 'what would you like to do more of?', 'what is less useful?', 'what would you like to change in the way we are working together?' And we need to remember that language matters, and is saturated with meaning which can distort or influence the interaction in ways we are not aware of in the moment of use. So, for instance, starting counselling with 'how can I be useful?', rather than 'how can I help?' moves away from an expert position and suggests a collaborative approach to the work. Avoiding any language that disempowers young people is essential, both when with young people and in our conversations about young people with others. Narrative counsellors take this further and many would not use the word 'client' – and it is not used in this chapter.

Practitioner reflections: Language that leads to labelling

When working as a career counsellor with young people under the age of 18 who were unemployed and unable to access full benefits, I visited the local unemployment office to see how we could improve the process of referring young people for the limited financial support that was available. The person I met welcomed me to her office, pointed to the bottom drawer of a filing cabinet (one in a bank of several) and said, 'That's where I keep all the files on the youngsters you send, you can see it is a small part of my work.' The drawer was labelled 'Kiddies Drawer'.

Her language was shaped by the professional context and the economic discourses within which she worked, but what does the above tell you about her view of young people and their needs? How do you think one of those 'youngsters' would feel visiting her in that context?

Of course, the questions suggested above, used to check the appropriateness of our interventions, are useful in any approach to counselling and nothing that is offered in this chapter should be viewed as a 'prescription' to be taken only with narrative counselling. It is important to note that narrative counselling (and even the singular term is problematic, as it suggests one way of using narrative in counselling) is drawn from broad cultural traditions and should not be viewed as a new way of 'delivering' counselling to young people. It would be a pointless task to search for a comprehensive cookbook or 'narrative handbook' (McLeod, 1997) on how to do this work. The approach is derived from what McLeod refers to as a distinctive philosophical and political position within counselling, and he warns against the therapeutic 'mining' of constructivist approaches. The assumptions that underpin a social constructivist view of the world and our place within it, mean a counsellor may need to do some rethinking about the nature of what is 'true', 'real' and 'meaningful', for both the young person and themselves. Michael White who, with others, led the development of narrative counselling suggests:

> *(the) running together of distinct traditions of thought and practice . . . leads to the false representation of the positions of different thinkers . . . when these distinctions are blurred we cannot find a place in which we may sit together, regardless of our different persuasions, and engage in conversations with each other in which we might all extend the limits of what we already think.*
>
> (White, 2000, pp103–4)

There is something in this quote that suggests 'good fences make for good neighbours'. Thus, it is important to be aware of the underpinning philosophy of the approach, but to be open to the possibility that *when properly understood* narrative thinking can be *introduced into other ways of working* (Payne, 2006, p6).

An important aspect of the narrative approach is to question who has the authority – the authorial voice, if you like – to tell the stories that are meaningful in counselling. As such narrative therapies can help to bridge the divide between approaches focused solely on the individual, rather than the individual operating in a social and cultural context. The aim is to provide a 'transitional space' (Winnicot, 1971) where the young person has the opportunity to tell their current story and to construct a new and different story. This can sound rather magical, but if we acknowledge that telling stories is evident in all societies as a fundamental means of communicating and developing understanding, then working alongside a young person to assist them to change a story from one that is 'bad' to one that is 'good' sounds less complicated. Such conversations are always undertaken with respectful curiosity, a respect that keeps the ethics of social justice (as outlined in Chapter 4 on multiculturalism) in the forefront of our work.

Young people are used to being on the receiving end of advice which pays little attention, however well intentioned, to their unspoken goals and aspirations. In contrast, narrative conversations provide a space for creativity and make room for a playfulness that is lacking in many approaches to the 'serious' work of counselling young people.

The narrative counsellor will have counselling skills, but believes that it makes sense, and is more likely to lead to effective practice, if great care is taken to understand the young person's knowledge of what would be meaningful action. Individual young people are not the sole authors of their stories and the focus on relations of power/knowledge within narrative therapy (informed by the work of Foucault, e.g. 1965, 1973, 1980) grounds the approach in the lived experiences of young people. Although the approach is optimistic and forward looking, it pays attention to the 'there and then' – *in context* – as well as the 'here and now'. In so doing it moves away from the language of deficit evident in many approaches to working with young people, where they are described by a litany of lacks, needs and faults; thus, different and more positive descriptions can be worked towards. Stories do more than describe; they can construct what we 'see' and how we react to the young person and their 'problem'.

> *We live our lives according to the stories we tell ourselves and the stories that others tell about us.*
>
> (Winslade and Monk, 2007, p2)

ACTIVITY 9.2

- How much of the previous discussion did you understand? Try summarising your understanding now, in three or four bullet points.

KEY CONCEPTS FOR NARRATIVE COUNSELLING WITH YOUNG PEOPLE

Before moving on to look at some of the activities used in narrative counselling, this section considers the key concepts that make it a particularly useful approach for counselling work with young people. Winslade and Monk (2007) have identified seven points based on their narrative approach for school counsellors, which they see as clarifying the distinctiveness of the approach. These are adapted and summarised in what follows.

- A common concern is that the narrative approach wallows in the dark corners of childhood dramas, but the approach is not about *long-term personality reconstruction* (Winslade and Monk, 2007, pix). When working with young people, rather than adults, we would not deny that they have childhood stories to tell, but they are still experiencing childhood, even though they are on the threshold of adulthood. Thus, the approach is more likely to be conducted in *a number of short counselling sessions*, rather than long-term therapy that examines childhood experiences in depth.

- The counsellor believes that the young person is the expert on their situation, not the counsellor.
- While the counsellor takes care to acknowledge feelings and emotions, and provides a safe space for these to be expressed, they do not act to provoke these as a route to change. The focus is on the young person's position in the story told and how they can separate their 'self' in a disabling problem story and identify their abilities: *to own their competence and resourcefulness or their capacity to find a solution [rather] than to take ownership of a problem* (Winslade and Monk, 2007, px). The *externalising* statement of Michael White (1989, p7) sums this up nicely: *The person is not the problem; the problem is the problem.* In avoiding blaming conversations, this does not mean that the counsellor colludes with behaviour and action that the young person needs to address. As this is such an important point, a case study may be useful here.

Case study 9.1   An invitation to take responsibility

Leo is a school counsellor who has an appointment with James, a 13-year-old student. He is told by the head of year that James 'is displaying a pattern of bullying and harassment towards girls in his year, which is increasing, despite disciplinary measures and conversations with parents'. Leo thinks that it will be helpful to avoid an approach that starts with any talk about the causes of the behaviour, or any blaming of James or others for what is happening. He wants to start the relationship with James (if indeed James comes for the appointment) by acknowledging that attending the meeting is a positive step. James does arrive – late, looking bored, sits in the chair and avoids eye contact with Leo. After introductions, Leo addresses the reason for the meeting.

Leo: 'Can you help me to understand, James, why you are here today?'
James: 'I'm only here 'cause I was told to come.'
Leo: 'I see. It must have taken courage to come through the door.'
James (surprised and looking at Leo for the first time): 'Not really.'
Leo: 'Many people regret things that they do that are hurtful to others and find it difficult to face up to what they have done. How come you are managing to do that?'
James: 'What do you mean?'

Leo: 'Well, what does it say about you, James, that you have started to face up to that by coming here today?'

James: (looking a bit confused) 'Dunno.'

Leo: 'I think it means that you are strong enough to face up to what you have done and that we can work together on this. Can you handle talking about your bullying?'

James: (shrugs) 'Yeah.'

Leo: 'What I'd like us to do first is to explore your beliefs about how to behave towards girls. Can we start there?'

COMMENT

What Leo is doing here is *inviting* (Jenkins, 1990) James to start taking responsibility for his actions and to make way for the development of an identity that moves away from that of bully. The conversation will continue by inviting James to explore respectful, non-abusive ways of relating to others. Questions could be asked about the kind of friendships James values; the type of relationships he would prefer to have with girls; how he feels about the way girls think about him at the moment and how he would like them to think of him. This could then lead on to what kind of relationship he would need to have with the girls in his year for them to think about him in those ways.

- Returning to the key concepts, a narrative approach does not only pay attention to the present. Stories are dynamic in that they have a past, a present and a future, and the point of present and future action needs to be meaningful for the individual. Ignoring the past is to discount the *abilities* of the young person and the resources that can be used in the counselling process.
- The chapter has already mentioned the importance of language and not making assumptions about the language we use. A narrative approach avoids technical language or jargon and pays attention to the language that the young person uses – in particular, the metaphors they use to express meaning. The counsellor uses those metaphors to join with the young person's language in their sense-making conversations. There may need to be a slight caution here as young people can react negatively to an adult who overuses their language in an attempt to be 'cool'.
- The approach does not separate the individual from their families, community and context. In contrast, it uses significant others as a resource to help the young person construct the new story and to act as an audience. In other words, every good story needs to be heard – requiring an appreciative audience for the young person to receive

wider feedback on the new identity, outside of the cocoon of the counselling space.

- It is not a coincidence that the work of White, and of Winslade and Monk, has already been introduced to the reader in the chapter on multiculturalism – narrative counselling does not assume a singular approach to counselling for psychological problems. With its focus on power/knowledge and the questioning of who is speaking in a story (and what the cultural influences may be in the tale told), it seeks to reveal the shaping effects of the stories, stories that are often scripted by more powerful 'others' in the lives of young people. Thus, the approach, rooted in respectful curiosity, can respond to the complexities of cultural diversities.

This chapter is limited in the amount of detail that can be devoted to what are sophisticated activities that need to be explored further and then practised. Nevertheless, as an introduction to the approach, what follows outlines certain practices that can be found in narrative counselling.

NARRATIVE IN PRACTICE

It is not the suggestion here that the practices outlined below will happen in a certain sequence or that they are always evident. And to emphasise an earlier point about the need for a proper understanding of the philosophical basis of narrative counselling, knowledgeable narrative practice requires more than the learning of a list of 'techniques' – so the word is not used here.

Listening to problem-saturated descriptions

Respectful curiosity, built through rapport, can only be respectful in a setting that is appropriate, where genuine listening and attending can take place. A young person may tell stories that are sad, disturbing or angry, which appear to contain nothing that is hopeful or positive in the telling. This is the story that is dominating their life at the present time and is what White described as a *problem-saturated description*. It is important that this story is 'heard' by the counsellor and taken seriously. At the same time, although the dominant story and the reason the young person is present are real, the 'problem' story does not encapsulate the whole of their life. The stories told at this point may need to be clarified so that the counsellor hears about the effects of these difficulties on the young person's life, as they see them. In time, the counsellor will want to hear a richer story about the young person, rather than what White later called a *thin description*.

Case study 9.2   Listening to the story

Carol is a youth counsellor working in the evening in an outreach centre at a youth club. Naz is 16 and has been brought by her friend Julie to see Carol. Julie says Naz is depressed and she is worried about her. Naz tells a sad story about arguments at home, a brother who steals to pay for drugs, time spent away from school to look after younger siblings and exam results that mean she cannot stay at the school. Naz's body language is tense and her tone of voice is despairing. She says that she feels she is 'depressed and living inside a black cloud'. Carol listens and is conscious of feeling how bleak Naz's situation is, but wants to ensure that she does not get 'bogged down' in the story. She listens carefully, but also attends to her own responses, ensuring they are empathic, but not over-positive, in an attempt to move Naz to the point where a richer description about Naz can be constructed.

But that is not for this evening – for now she builds trust and rapport, checking out that Naz is not in danger, and maintaining her respect for how 'depression' is causing difficulties in Naz's life. She does not offer interpretations about what is happening, as she assumes Naz is the expert on this. She acknowledges in her responses to Naz, that the courage to tell others her story shows that she has the ability to loosen the grip of 'depression'. She avoids thinking about Naz only in terms of her depression. Naz (who feels she has been listened to and understood) agrees to meet with Carol the next day.

Listening is the key to effectiveness in the above example, but it is not listening to find solutions at this early stage. We will return to the stories of both Naz and James, as we explore other narrative practices.

Naming and externalising the problem

Naming the problem is a key step in separating the person from the problem. The counsellor will pay attention to the young person's language, but if they cannot think of a name to make the problem a 'thing', separate from them as a person, a provisional name can be agreed at the beginning. In Naz's story the counsellor uses 'depression' – a more precise name may emerge later. This is the first step in the process of externalising the problem. In different circumstances 'trouble' can be a useful name at the start of the counselling relationship.

The point of externalising language is to establish the standpoint that the problem is having an effect on the person, rather than being an intrinsic part of the person caused by their psychology or a personality trait.

For example, Carol would say, 'Tell me, Naz, how depression affects your life.' She would not say, 'So, you have become depressed, tell me about that Naz.' Returning to a point made earlier, externalising language is not used for abusive actions; these are named directly. So, in the earlier story with the young person James, Leo would say, 'You have bullied the girls over a long period now.' However, the beliefs and assumptions about relationships with girls can be examined through an externalising conversation, 'From what you have said James, you are acting from a belief that bullying girls is acceptable – can we look at how that belief affects the current situation and influences Trouble?' Other examples that can be used as appropriate to the situation could be Anger, or Failure; for instance, 'So, Anger got you to shout at the teacher . . .' not 'You were angry and . . .' or 'What influence is Failure having on you at the moment?' not 'How do you feel about failing that exam?'

In narrative counselling, a settled name (thus a noun, not a verb) for the problem may take a while to emerge and, of course, may change. The counsellor should not rush into looking for the name before they have listened to a full exploration of the problem. Externalising conversations evolve over time and 'naming' needs to be flexible as the young person and their situation change. In any activity that feels odd to the counsellor at the first attempt (and probably to the young person, too), the solution is to be open and share what you are doing. For example, 'I find it is useful sometimes to talk about the problem as if it is outside of you and then explore how it is affecting you. This can help us to see it from a different angle and find ways to deal with it. Is it OK if we have a go talking about it in this way?' If there are multiple problems, then the young person and the counsellor will need to agree which issue is the one to address first. A final point here, naming needs to externalise the problem, so a name for an eating disorder located in a view of self as 'too fat', would need careful thought. Binge Eating as a label internalises the problem as it suggests a lack of will-power – a more useful name could be linked to the person's views about body image, for instance, Catwalk Look.

In thinking about the effects of the problem, questions can be asked which *map* (White, 2007) these in terms of length (how long?; the problem's history), breadth (the spread of the problem's effects; in and out of school and so on) and depth (the intensity of the influence of the problem). Mapping during the course of counselling should help to chart changes and can help with focusing the work.

Discovering clues on competence

The kind of deep listening required in this approach is hard work (but worth the effort). As the counselling continues, the counsellor is alert to discover any clues to identify the young person's competence. Winslade and Monk (2007, p50) refer to this as *detective work*, looking to find evidence where none may appear on the surface level of the story. To the client, and a counsellor not involved in this deep listening, these clues can pass unobserved, but if the counsellor *combs carefully through the problem-saturated story* they can find an *opening to a different story* (Winslade and Monk, 2007, p50). Such clues need to be picked up and developed in the conversation. White and Epston (1990) described these as *unique outcomes* related to:

- *actions;*
- *thoughts;*
- *intentions to act;*
- *moments when the effects of the problem don't seem so strong;*
- *areas of life that remain unaffected by the problem;*
- *special abilities;*
- *knowledge about how to overcome the problem;*
- *problem-free responses from others;*
- *relationships that defy the problem's persuasions.*

(Winslade and Monk, 2007, p50)

If we return to Naz's story, Carol might ask, 'Tell me about the times when Depression does not keep you in that black cloud.' Or 'Although Depression wants you to stay in bed, how do you beat it and still get out and about?' Or 'Despite Depression's influence on you – how is it that you have not given in and are here talking with me?' The aim is to look for an opening into a more hopeful story.

ACTIVITY 9.3

- Think about a young person you have worked with recently. How did you talk about the presenting problem? What language did you use? How could you move to externalising conversations, looking also for clues of their competence?
- Write down the actual words and phrases that you could use in a similar situation. If you have any of your interviews recorded (with permission from the young person) look for signs of where the problem is internalised (made part of the person) and think about phrases that could externalise the problem (separate from the person). Is there any hidden evidence of competence?

Working with the alternative story

Elsewhere in this book we have talked about working towards goals and ensuring that the goals are owned by the young person. The same principles apply in narrative work when working alongside a young person to develop and work with the alternative story for their life. Within the narrative approach, the counsellor works collaboratively with the young person to assist them to reflect on *whether they would like to participate in living their lives according to ongoing problem-saturated narratives or according to alternate, preferred narratives* (Winslade and Monk, 2007, p59). This will take time and the counsellor and the young person need to persist and not 'run out of steam'.

> *Just as the problem story has grown in strength, so must the alternative story develop a plot that is robust enough to stand up to the problem story's authority.*
>
> (Winslade and Monk, 2007, p60)

Authority is an interesting word in terms of storytelling. The authorial voice (the powerful voice(s) that can be heard in the story) needs to move from the problem being in control and determining the narration, to the young person being enabled to take control. But, without taking over, the counsellor will need to be active at this stage to avoid the process floundering. Speedy (2008, p61) explains that in narrative counselling the point is not to gather data for later analysis, but to *support people in noticing they are making a difference to the stories they tell about themselves* there and then, *in the conversation, and thus, the way they live their lives*. Returning to James and Leo, the case study summarises the story so far and then moves to working with an alternative story. How does the story about James change in the *there and then?*

Case study 9.3   James and Leo move on to work with an alternative story

Leo avoided naming the problem as Bullying as that could revert back to the dominant story about James: they decided to use Trouble. Leo and James have worked together on ways to counter Trouble's influence on James. In their conversations, they talked about Trouble's behaviour and how powerful Trouble makes James feel; his (James's) reputation with some of his friends; other voices or cultural stories about 'not being a wimp' and so on. James also described the type of relationships he would like to have with girls, if he could loosen Trouble's influence on him. They also thought about the future.

Leo: 'I want to think now about your reputation in the school, James. If things keep getting worse, where do you think they could end up?'
James: 'I dunno – I might get chucked out of school, I suppose.'
Leo: 'Is this the direction you want things to take?'
James: 'Not really.'
Leo: 'Tell me why not, James.'

Rather than concentrate on what is causing James's behaviour, Leo asks questions to examine what is stopping the desired change from happening. Having separated the problem from the person, they went on to identify numerous tactics for outsmarting Trouble, drawing on resources from times when Trouble was not in control. James talked about his cousin Zoe who he 'gets on with', because he knows her well. They spent time thinking about what was involved in getting on well with Zoe, what he liked about her company and how he could use these thoughts when Trouble wanted him to bully the girls in his year. Another story about James emerged. Both James and Zoe are 'a bit arty' and, following up on this clue, Leo finds out that in art lessons in school Trouble does not bother James so much. They work with this positive reputation some more, thinking about how Arty James can ignore Trouble. Leo says he would like to see some of James's art work.

Things have started to improve in school and Leo meets with James again. Today, James brings a folder of work that impresses and surprises Leo.

Leo: 'James, this work is great – look how delicate the drawing is here!'
James: 'It's OK.'
Leo: 'OK! Has Zoe seen this work?'
James: 'No, it's just school stuff.'
Leo: 'You mean you have more work at home?'
James: 'Yeah.'
Leo: 'Who else has seen this in school, other than your art teacher?'
James: 'Some of the others in the class.'
Leo: 'Who would that be then?'
James: 'Prem, Tracey and Clare – we work on the same table.'
Leo: 'And how do you all work together – how do you get on?'
James: 'Good, we were all talking yesterday about doing something in art together after year 11.'
Leo: 'What do you think the head of year would think about this conversation we are having now, James, now that you are starting to drive the old Trouble out of your life?'

COMMENT

The conversations with Leo help James to think about himself and others in a different and more positive way. Of course, real stories in real lives are rarely straightforward and life is inclined to be messy, complex rather than simple. The above case study is an episode in a narrative. In Chapter 7 on motivational interviewing, 'relapse' was highlighted as a normal part of change. When moving forward there are many places where a young person can stumble, when the old story 'rears up' and previous patterns of behaviour reappear, particularly in times of stress. As with any approach in counselling, it is useful to rehearse a number of strategies that can help manage difficulties and relapse in preparation for when it may occur. This can also include drawing on the help of a wider audience who want to support the alternative story.

Documenting the evidence and engaging an audience in the new story

When constructing a preferred story, saying it 'out loud' helps it to become real. An alternative story begins to feel successful when it is appreciated by others. In narrative counselling the counsellor and the young person reach a point when they are alert to how others might undermine the structure of the new story. Others outside of the counselling room may not have witnessed the change and are expecting behaviour that fits with the old story. Thus, in narrative work, the counsellor will pay attention to the wider context of the young person, to engage others as an audience to witness and support the development of the alternative story. The creation of written documents and statements can help, but these need to be meaningful for both the young person and the target audience, so they must be thought through carefully with the young person. It is also normal practice for the counsellor to write a letter to the young person celebrating their achievements. Here is a letter Carol wrote to Naz, nearing the end of their work together.

Practitioner reflections: A letter from Carol to Naz

Dear Naz,

I wanted to write down my thoughts after our conversation yesterday and send these to you. I found myself reflecting on the possibilities that are now opening up for you at this moment. You used the words 'opening up' when talking about how that cloud no longer encloses you all of the time and, even when it does, it is no longer black. When I asked you what colour it was you said, 'Silvery grey, with black edges at times.' You said that recently Depression was finding it much more difficult to get in the way of your plans and that you had nearly completed the application form for the course at college that you want to do.

It was a privilege for me to hear about your plans. Thank you for bringing in the prospectus and telling me what you had found out about the course and where you want it to lead. I enjoyed your story about where you see yourself in the future, particularly the part about the travel involved. I was really struck by your resourcefulness in arranging this and the energy you spoke with. It took courage

---

to make the appointment and visit that tutor at a college you had not been to before, the sort of courage that you have demonstrated recently, during a difficult time.

You said that Depression still lurks in the shadows and you spoke about how you can identify some of the signs that Depression is asserting itself. How are you getting on with the strategies we developed? Thank you, Naz, for sharing your story with me. I can't wait for the next chapter!

With warm wishes, Carol

CHAPTER SUMMARY

This final chapter has explored some of the ideas that have led to the development of narrative counselling and considered the key concepts that distinguish narrative from other kinds of counselling. It has looked at practices that might be incorporated into work with young people and suggested that these could be integrated within the reflexive practitioner's counselling model. It has warned against a blind 'pick and mix' approach, but has suggested that knowledge of discrete counselling approaches (narrative being one among others) can help us to see where the common ground lies. Looking beyond therapeutic boundaries can help us to view that common ground as a place for challenging practice and learning from different approaches. This seems more productive than viewing the space in between as a 'no man's land', difficult and dangerous to traverse.

SUGGESTED FURTHER READING

At the start of this chapter it was stated that it is important to be aware of the underpinning philosophy of the approach, but to be open to the possibility that *when properly understood* narrative thinking can be *introduced into other ways of working* (Payne, 2006, p6). To achieve that, the following books are recommended.

Payne, M (2006) *Narrative Therapy: An Introduction for Counsellors,* 2nd edition. London: Sage.

An excellent review of narrative therapy which explains the underpinning theory and applies this to practice examples.

McLeod, J (1997) *Narrative and Psychotherapy*. London: Sage.

This work helps to place narrative therapy within the historical and cultural roots of psychotherapy and takes a critical approach, drawing on extensive knowledge and research. Again, case vignettes and examples are excellent.

Speedy, J (2008) *Narrative Inquiry and Psychotherapy*. Hampshire: Palgrave Macmillan.

Engaging and creative with many interesting case studies, this book considers narrative and life story in research settings, leading to insights into different kinds of questions that are relevant to counselling practice. Its creativity crosses the boundaries between therapy and 'art'.

Winslade, J and Monk, G (2007) *Narrative Counseling in Schools: Powerful and Brief*, 2nd edition. Thousand Oaks, California: Corwin Press.

Accessible and particularly useful for working with young people, with outstanding examples and case studies. An essential read.

White, M (2007) *Maps of Narrative Practice*. New York: Norton & Co.

Seminal, and a detailed and compelling guide for practice. It includes moving stories to illustrate the approach in practice.

Conclusion

The various approaches that have been presented to you in this book all have one aim – to engage young people in conversations that open up opportunities in their lives for growth. Counselling conversations are not linear and ordered in the way they are presented on paper. Whatever you are applying, be intentional – understand what it is that you are doing, but make room for flexibility, for adaptability and serendipity. Also, accept that you never stop learning from young people and from others. Michael White was a modest man who did not see himself as the architect of narrative counselling, but as a contributor to its ongoing development. He wrote:

> *To date, there has not been one occasion on which I could say that I wouldn't change some aspect of my contribution to a therapeutic conversation if I had the opportunity to start all over again. This acknowledgment is not to negatively judge or devalue my part in these conversations, and it does not subtract from the enjoyment that I experience in them. Rather, it is about maintaining a reflective perspective on what I do as a therapist.*
> (2007, p7)

Working with young people in any context can be challenging, but the resilience and resources of young people should never be underestimated. If we attend to our own development as counsellors and remain optimistic in the work, then counselling young people is, in most cases, a rewarding and uplifting experience.

References

Allen, NB and Sheeber, LB (2008) *Adolescent Emotional Development and the Emergence of Depressive Disorders.* Cambridge: Cambridge University Press.

Arnett, JJ (1999) Adolescent storm and stress, reconsidered. *American Psychologist,* 54 (5): 317–326.

Arulmani, G (2009) A matter of culture. *Career Guidance Today*, Institute of Career Guidance, 17(1), March: 0–12.

Balint, M, Ornstein, PO and Balint, E (1972) *Focal Psychotherapy.* London: Tavistock.

Bandura, A (1977) *Social Learning Theory.* Englewood Cliffs, NJ: Prentice-Hall.

Barenboim, C (1981) The development of person perception in childhood and adolescence. *Child Development,* 52: 129–144.

Barrett-Kruse, C (1994) Brief counselling: a user's guide for traditionally trained counsellors. *International Journal for the Advancement of Counselling,* 17: 109–115.

Beck, A (1976) *Cognitive Therapy and the Emotional Disorders.* New York: International University Press.

Berne, E (1964) *Games People Play.* Middlesex: Penguin.

Besley, T (2002) *Counseling Youth: Foucault, Power and the Ethics of Subjectivity.* Westport, CA: Praeger.

Beven, P (2009) Client narratives, language and motivation, in Reid, HL (ed.) *Constructing the Future: Career Guidance for Changing Contexts.* Stourbridge, UK: Institute of Career Guidance – available on www.icg-uk.org/publications

Bion, WR (1970) *Attention and Interpretation.* London: Tavistock.

Bimrose, J (1996) Multiculturalism, in Bayne, R, Horton, I and Bimrose, J (eds) *New Directions in Counselling.* London: Routledge.

Bond, T (2010) *Standards and Ethics for Counselling in Action* (3rd edition). London: Sage.

Bordin, E (1979) The generalisability of the psychoanalytic concept and the working alliance. *Psychotherapy: Theory, Research and Practice,* 16: 252–260.

Bowlby, J (1969) *Attachment and Loss, Vol 1: Attachment.* New York: Basic Books.

Boyd, D and Bee, H (2009) *Lifespan Development,* 5th edition. Boston: Pearson.

Britzman, D (2000) The question of belief: writing poststructural ethnography, in St Pierre, EA and Pillow, W (eds) *Working the*

Ruins: Feminist Poststructural Theory and Methods in Education. New York: Routledge.

Brooks-Gunn, J and Petersen, AC (1984) Problems in studying and defining pubertal events. *Journal of Youth and Adolescence,* 13: 181–196.

Bruner, J (1990) *Acts of Meaning.* Cambridge, Massachusetts: Harvard University Press.

Christie, D and Viner, R (2005) Adolescent development, in Viner, R (ed.) *ABC of Adolescence.* Oxford: Blackwell.

Claringbull, N (2010) *What is Counselling and Psychotherapy?* Exeter: Learning Matters.

Clarkson, P (2003) *The Therapeutic Relationship,* 2nd edition. London: Whurr.

Clarkson, P (2005) *On Psychotherapy: Vol 4.* London: John Wiley and Sons.

Coleman, J and Hendry, LB (1999) *The Nature of Adolescence,* 3rd edition. London: Routledge.

Collander-Brown, D (2005) Being with another as a professional practitioner: uncovering the nature of working with individuals. *Youth and Policy,* 86: 33–47.

Colledge, R (2002) *Mastering Counselling Theory.* Hampshire: Palgrave Macmillan.

Cooper, M and McLeod, J (2010) *Pluralistic Counselling and Psychotherapy.* London: Sage.

Cornell, WF and Hargarden, H (eds) (2005) *The Emergence of a Relational Tradition in Transactional Analysis.* Oxford: Haddon Press.

Culley, S and Bond, T (2004) *Integrative Counselling Skills in Action.* London: Sage.

Daniels, D and Jenkins, P (2010) *Therapy with Children: Children's Rights, Confidentiality and the Law,* 2nd edition. London: Sage.

Department of Health (2008) *Improving Access to Psychological Therapies Implementation Plan: National Guidelines for Regional Delivery.* Nottingham: DH.

de Shazer, S, Berg, IK, Lipchik, E, Nunnally, E, Molnar, A, Gingerich, W and Weiner-Davis, M (1986) Brief therapy: focused solution development. *Family Process,* 25: 207–221.

de Shazer, S (1988) *Clues: Investigating Solutions in Brief Therapy.* New York: WW Norton.

DiClemente, CC and Velasquez, M (2002) Motivational interviewing and the stages of change, in Miller, WR and Rollnick, R (eds) *Motivational Interviewing: Preparing People for Change,* 2nd edition. New York: The Guilford Press.

Dryden, W (2005) *Overcoming Jealousy.* London: Sheldon Press.

Dryden, W and Feltham, C (1992) *Brief Counselling: A Practical Guide for Beginning Practitioners.* Buckingham: Open University Press.

Egan, G (2002) *The Skilled Helper: A Problem-Management and Opportunity-Development Approach to Helping,* 7th edition. Pacific Grove: Brooks/Cole.

Egan, G (2007) *The Skilled Helper: A Problem-Management and Opportunity-Development Approach to Helping,* 8th edition. Pacific Grove, California: Brooks/Cole.

Elkind, D (1967) Egocentrism in adolescence. *Child Development*. 38: 1025–1034.

Ellis, A (1962) *Reason and Emotion in Psychotherapy*. New York: Lyle Stuart.

Ellis, A (1989) The history of cognition in psychotherapy, in Freeman, A, Simon, KM, Beutler, LE and Arkowitz, H (eds) *Comprehensive Handbook of Cognitive Therapy*. New York: Plenum Press.

Ellis, A (2001) *Overcoming Destructive Beliefs, Feelings and Behaviours: New Directions for Rational Emotive Therapy*. Amherst, New York: Prometheus Books.

Erikson, EH (1968) *Identity: Youth and Crisis*. New York: WW Norton.

Etherington, K (2004) *Becoming a Reflexive Researcher*. London: Jessica Kingsley Publishers.

Evans, K and Gilbert, M (2005) *Introduction to Integrative Psychotherapy*. Basingstoke: Palgrave Macmillan.

Eysenk, HJ (1970) A mish-mash of theories. *International Journal of Psychiatry*, 9: 140–146.

Flegenheimer, WV (1982) *Techniques of Brief Psychotherapy*. New York: Aronson.

Foucault, M (1965) *Madness and Civilization: A History of Insanity in the Age of Reason*. New York: Random House.

Foucault, M (1973) *The Birth of the Clinic: An Archaeology of Medical Perception*. London: Tavistock.

Foucault, M (1980) *Power/Knowledge: Selected Interviews and Other Writings 1972–1977*. London: Harvester Press.

Geldard, K and Geldard, D (2004) *Counselling Adolescents*, 2nd edition. London: Sage.

Geldard, K and Geldard, D (2009) *Counselling Adolescents*, 3rd edition. London: Sage.

Gergen, KJ (1994) *Reality and Relationships: Soundings in Social Construction*. Cambridge, MA: Harvard University Press.

Green, J (2010) *Creating the Therapeutic Relationship in Counselling and Psychotherapy*. Exeter: Learning Matters.

Greenberger, D and Padesky, C (1995) *Mind Over Mood*. New York: Guilford Press.

Harris, T (1995) *I'm OK – You're OK*. Reading: Arrow Books.

Jenkins, A (1990) *Invitations to Responsibility: The Therapeutic Engagement of Men who are Violent and Abusive*. Adelaide, Australia: Dulwich Centre Publications.

Jenkins, P (2000) Gerard Egan's skilled helper model, in Palmer, S and Woolfe, R (eds) *Integrative and Eclectic Counselling and Psychotherapy*. London: Sage.

Kaplan, PS (2004) *Adolescence*. Boston: Houghton Mifflin.

Keating, DP (1991) Adolescent cognition, in Lerner, RM, Petersen, AC and Brooks-Gunn, J (eds) *Encyclopaedia of Adolescence*. New York: Garland.

Kelly, G (1955) *The Psychology of Personal Constructs, Volumes 1 and 2*. New York: WW Norton.

Kennedy, E and Charles, SC (2002) *On Becoming a Counsellor: A Basic Guide for Non-Professional Counsellors,* 3rd edition. Cheshire: Newleaf.

Kincheloe, JL and Steinberg, SF (1997) *Changing Multiculturalism.* Buckingham: Open University Press.

Kohlberg, L (ed.) (1984) *The Psychology of Moral Development: Vol. 2.* San Francisco: Harper and Row.

Kuyken, W (2005) Research and evidence base in case formulation, in Tarrier, N (ed.) *Case Formulation in Cognitive Behaviour Therapy: The Treatment of Challenging and Complex Clinical Cases.* Hove: Brunner-Routledge.

Larson, R, Csikzentmihalyi, M and Graef, R (1980) Mood variability and the psychosocial adjustment of adolescents. *Journal of Youth and Adolescence.* New York: Garland. 9: 469–490.

Lazarus, AA (1995) Different types of eclecticism and integration: let's be aware of the dangers, *Journal of Psychotherapy Integration,* 5 (1): 27–39.

Leadbetter, B (1991) Relativistic thinking in adolescence, in Lerner, RM, Petersen, AC and Brooks-Gunn, J (eds) *Encyclopaedia of Adolescence.* New York: Garland.

Leahy, RL (2003) *Cognitive Therapy Techniques.* New York: Guilford Press.

Levitas, R (2005) *The Inclusive Society? Social Exclusion and New Labour,* 2nd edition. Hampshire: Macmillan Press.

Lines, D (2006) *Brief Counselling in Schools: Working with Young People from 11 to 18,* 2nd edition. London: Sage.

Lister-Ford, C (2002) *Skills in Transactional Analysis Counselling and Psychotherapy.* London: Sage.

Malan, DH (1975) *A Study of Brief Psychotherapy.* London: Plenum.

Mallon, B (2010) *Working with Bereaved Children and Young People.* London: Sage.

Marcia, JE (1966) Development and validation of ego identity status. *Journal of Personality and Social Psychology,* 3: 551–558.

Marcia, JE (1980) Identity in adolescence, in Adelson, J (ed.) *Handbook of Adolescent Psychology.* New York: Wiley.

McLeod, J (1997) *Narrative and Psychotherapy.* London: Sage.

McLeod, J (1998) *An Introduction to Counselling,* 2nd edition. Buckingham: Open University Press.

McLeod, J (2003) *An Introduction to Counselling,* 3rd edition. Buckingham: Open University Press.

McLeod, J (2004) *The Counsellor's Workbook: Developing a Personal Approach.* Berkshire: Open University Press.

McLeod, J (2009) *An Introduction to Counselling,* 4th edition. Buckingham: Open University Press.

McMaster, F and Kusumakar, V (2004) MRI study of the pituitary gland in adolescent depression. *Journal of Psychiatric Research,* 38: 231–236.

Mearns, D and Cooper, M (2005) *Working at Relational Depth in Counselling and Psychotherapy.* London: Sage.

Mearns, D and Thorne, B (2000) *Person-centred Therapy Today.* London: Sage.

Miller, WR and Rollnick, R (2002) *Motivational Interviewing: Preparing People for Change*, 2nd edition. New York: The Guilford Press.

Monk, G, Winslade, J and Sinclair, S (2008) *New Horizons in Multicultural Counselling*. Thousand Oaks, California: Sage Publications.

Myers, S (2007) *Solution-focused Approaches (Theory into Practice)*. Dorset: Russell House Publishing.

O'Brien, M and Houston, G (2000) *Integrative Therapy*. London: Sage.

O'Connell, B (2001) *Solution-Focused Stress Counselling*. London: Continuum.

O'Connell, B (2005) *Solution-Focused Therapy*, 2nd edition. London: Sage.

Orlinsky, D, Grawe, K and Parks, BK (1994) Process and outcome in psychotherapy – noch einmal, in Bergin, AE and Garfield, SL (eds) *Handbook of Psychotherapy and Behavior Change,* 4th edition. Chichester: Wiley.

Parker, I (2007) *Revolution in Psychology: Alienation to Emancipation*. London: Pluto Press.

Parsons, C (2009) Explaining sustained inequalities in ethnic minority school exclusions in England – passive racism in a neoliberal grip. *Oxford Review of Education*, 35(2): 249–265.

Pavlov, IP (1927) *Conditioned Reflexes: An Investigation of the Physiological Activity of the Cerebral Cortex*. translated and edited by Anrep, GV. London: Oxford University Press.

Payne, M (2006) *Narrative Therapy: An Introduction for Counsellors*, 2nd edition. London: Sage.

Piaget, J (1954) *The Construction of Reality in the Child*. New York: Basic Books.

Piaget, J (1977) *The Development of Thought: Equilibration of Cognitive Structures*. New York: Viking.

Prever, M (2010) *Counselling and Supporting Children and Young People: A Person-Centred Approach*. London: Sage.

Prochaska, JO and DiClemente, CC (1982) Transtheoretical therapy: Toward a more integrative model of change. *Psychotherapy: Theory, Research, and Practice*, 19: 276–288.

Reid, HL (2005) Beyond the toolbox: integrating multicultural principles into a career guidance intervention model, in Irving, BA and Malik, B (eds.) *Critical Reflections on Career Education and Guidance: Promoting Social Justice within a Global Economy*. London: RoutledgeFalmer.

Reid, HL (2008) Career guidance for 'at risk' young people: constructing a way forward, in Athanasou, JA and Van Esbroeck, R (eds) *International Handbook of Career Guidance*. Dordrecht: Springer: 461–485.

Reid, HL and Westergaard, J (eds) (2006) *Providing Support and Supervision: An Introduction for Professionals Working with Young People*. London: RoutledgeFalmer.

Reid, HL and Bassot, B (2011) Reflection: a constructive space for career development, in McMahon, M and Watson, M (eds) *Career Counselling and Constructivism: Elaboration of Constructs*. New York: Nova Publishers.

Roberts, K (2005) Social class, opportunity, structures and career guidance, in Irving, BA and Malik, B (eds) *Critical Reflections on Career Education and Guidance: Promoting Social Justice within a Global Economy*. London: RoutledgeFalmer.

Rogers, CR (1951) *Client-Centred Therapy*. Boston: Houghton Mifflin.

Rogers, CR (1967) *On Becoming a Person: A Therapist's View of Psychotherapy*. London: Constable.

Rollnick, S, Butler, CC, Kinnersley, P, Gregory, J and Mash, B (2010) Motivational Interviewing. *British Medical Journal*, 340:c1900, available on www.stephenrollnick.com/index.php/commentary/34-commentary-on-mi

Rollnick, S, and Miller, WR (1995) What is motivational interviewing? *Behavioural & Cognitive Psychotherapy*, 23: 325–334.

Rosenblum, GD and Lewis, M (1999) The relations among body image, physical attractiveness and body mass in adolescence. *Child Development*, 70: 50–64.

Rosenblum, GD and Lewis, M (2003) Emotional development in adolescence, in Adams, GR and Berzonsky, MD (eds) (2003) *Blackwell Handbook of Adolescence*. Malden, MA: Blackwell.

Roth, A and Fonagy, P (1996) *What Works for Whom? A Critical Review of Psychotherapy Research*. New York: Guilford Press.

Saltzman, C, Luetgert, MJ, Roth, CH, Creaser, J and Howard, L (1976) Formation of a therapeutic relationship: experiences during the initial phase of psychotherapy as predictors of treatment duration and outcome. *Journal of Consulting and Clinical Psychology*, 44: 546–555.

Saluja, G, Iachan, R, Scheidt, P, Overpeck, M, Sun, W and Giedd, J (2004) Prevalence of and risk factors for depressive symptoms among young adolescents. *Archives of Paediatric and Adolescent Medicine*, 158: 760–765.

Sanders, D and Wills, F (2005) *Cognitive Therapy: An Introduction*. London: Sage.

Schön, D (1983) *The Reflective Practitioner*. New York: Basic Books.

Seligman, MEP (1975) *Helplessness*. San Francisco: Freeman.

Selman, RL (1980) *The Growth of Interpersonal Understanding*. New York: Academic Press.

Shayer, M and Wylam, H (1978) The distribution of Piagetian stages of thinking in British middle and secondary school children: 2. *British Journal of Educational Psychology*, 48: 62–70.

Sheldon, B (1995) *Cognitive Behavioural Therapy: Research, Practice and Philosophy*. London: Routledge.

Simmons, J and Griffiths, R (2009) *CBT for Beginners*. London: Sage.

Skinner, BF (1953) *Science and Human Behavior*. New York: Macmillan.

Sklare, GB (2005) *Brief Counselling That Works: A Solution-Focused Approach for School Counsellors and Administrators*, 2nd edition. Thousand Oaks, California: Corwin Press.

Speedy, J (2008) *Narrative Inquiry and Psychotherapy*. Hampshire: Palgrave Macmillan.

Steinberg, L (1996) *Adolescence*, 4th edition. New York: McGraw-Hill.

Steiner, C (1990) *Scripts People Live: Transactional Analysis of Life Scripts,* 2nd edition. New York: Grove Press.

Stewart, I (2000) *Transactional Analysis in Action,* 2nd edition. London: Sage.

Stewart, I and Joines, V (1987) *TA Today. A New Introduction to Transactional Analysis.* Kegworth: Lifespace Publishing.

Sue, DW, Arrendondon, P and McDavis, RJ (1995) Multicultural counseling competencies and standards: a call to the profession, in Ponterotto, JG, Casas, JM, Suzuki, LA and Alexander, CM (eds) *Handbook of Multicultural Counseling.* California: Sage.

Sue, DW, Allen, EI and Pederson, PB (1996) *A Theory of Multicultural Counseling and Therapy.* Pacific Grove: Brooks/Cole.

Sutton, J and Stewart, W (2002) *Learning to Counsel: Develop the Skills You Need to Counsel Others.* Oxford: How To Books.

Szasz, T (1978) *The Myth of Psychotherapy.* Oxford: Oxford University Press.

Tanner, JM (1970) Physical growth, in Mussen, PH (ed.) *Carmichael's Manual of Child Development,* 3rd edition. New York: Wiley.

Thompson, N (1993) *Anti-Discriminatory Practice.* London: Macmillan.

Townend, A (2007) *Assertiveness and Diversity.* Hampshire: Palgrave Macmillan.

Transactional Analysis Journal, The International Transactional Analysis Association, California: USA (published quarterly).

Trower, P, Jones, J, Dryden, W and Casey, A (2011) *Cognitive Behavioural Counselling in Action*, 2nd edition. London: Sage.

Tudor, L, Keemar, K, Tudor, K, Valentine, J and Worrall, M (2004) *The Person-Centred Approach: A Contemporary Introduction.* Basingstoke: Palgrave Macmillan.

Turiel, E (1978) The development of concepts of social structure, in Glick, J and Clarke-Stewart, K (eds) *The Development of Social Understanding.* Gardner: New York.

Valliant, PM and Antonowicz DH (1991) Cognitive behaviour therapy and social skills training improves personality and cognition in incarcerated offenders. *Psychological Reports.* 68: 27–33.

Ward, E, King, M, Lloyd, M, Bower, P, Sibbald, B, Farrelly, S, Gabbay, M, Tarrier, N and Addington-Hall, J (2008) Randomised controlled trial of non-directive counselling, cognitive-behavioural therapy and usual general practitioner care for patients with depression. *British Medical Journal.* 321: 1383–1388.

Watson, JB (1919) *Psychology from the Standpoint of a Behaviourist.* Philadelphia: JB Lippincott.

White, M (1989) The externalisation of the problem and the re-authoring of relationships, in White, M *Selected Papers.* Adelaide, South Australia: Dulwich Centre Publications.

White, M (2000) *Reflections on Narrative Practice.* Adelaide, South Australia: Dulwich Centre Publications.

White, M (2007) *Maps of Narrative Practice.* New York: WW Norton.

White, M and Epston, D (1990) *Narrative Means to Therapeutic Ends*. New York: Norton.

Widdowson, M (2009) *Transactional Analysis: 100 Key Points and Techniques*. London: Routledge.

Wilkins, P (2001) Unconditional positive regard reconsidered, in Bozarth, JD and Wilkins, P (eds) *Rogers' Therapeutic Conditions: Evolution, Theory and Practice – Unconditional Positive Regard*. Ross-on-Wye: PCCS Books.

Wills, F (2008) *Cognitive Behaviour Counselling and Psychotherapy*. London: Sage.

Winnicott, D (1965) *The Maturation Process and the Facilitating Environment: Studies in the Theory of Emotional Development*. London: Hogarth Press.

Winnicott, D (1971) *Playing and Reality*. London: Routledge.

Winslade, J and Monk, G (2007) *Narrative Counseling in Schools: Powerful and Brief*, 2nd edition. Thousand Oaks, California: Corwin Press.

Winslade, J and Monk, G (2008) *Practicing Narrative Mediation: Loosening the Grip of Conflict*. San Francisco: Jossey-Bass.

Wolpe, J (1958) Cognition and causation in human behaviour and its therapy. *American Psychologist*. 33: 437–446.

Wosket, V (2006) *Egan's Skilled Helper Model*. London: Routledge.

Index